ACTS

Chapters 15—28

J. Vernon McGee

THOMAS NELSON PUBLISHERS

Nashville

Published in Nashville, Tennessee, by Thomas Nelson, Inc., and distributed in Canada by Lawson Falle, Ltd., Cambridge, Ontario.

Scripture quotations are from the KING JAMES VERSION of the Bible.

Library of Congress Cataloging-in-Publication Data

McGee, J. Vernon (John Vernon), 1904–1988
   [Thru the Bible with J. Vernon McGee]
   Thru the Bible commentary series / J. Vernon McGee.
     p.   cm.
   Reprint. Originally published: Thru the Bible with J. Vernon McGee. 1975.
   Includes bibliographical references.
   ISBN 0-8407-3292-9
   1. Bible—Commentaries. I. Title.
BS491.2.M37   1991
220.7′7—dc20   90–41340
                           CIP

Printed in the United States of America
1 2 3 4 5 6 7 — 96 95 94 93 92 91

CONTENTS

ACTS—Chapters 15—28

PREFACE

The radio broadcasts of the Thru the Bible Radio five-year program were transcribed, edited, and published first in single-volume paperbacks to accommodate the radio audience.

There has been a minimal amount of further editing for this publication. Therefore, these messages are not the word-for-word recording of the taped messages which went out over the air. The changes were necessary to accommodate a reading audience rather than a listening audience.

These are popular messages, prepared originally for a radio audience. They should not be considered a commentary on the entire Bible in any sense of that term. These messages are devoid of any attempt to present a theological or technical commentary on the Bible. Behind these messages is a great deal of research and study in order to interpret the Bible from a popular rather than from a scholarly (and too-often boring) viewpoint.

We have definitely and deliberately attempted "to put the cookies on the bottom shelf so that the kiddies could get them."

The fact that these messages have been translated into many languages for radio broadcasting and have been received with enthusiasm reveals the need for a simple teaching of the whole Bible for the masses of the world.

I am indebted to many people and to many sources for bringing this volume into existence. I should express my especial thanks to my secretary, Gertrude Cutler, who supervised the editorial work; to Dr. Elliott R. Cole, my associate, who handled all the detailed work with the publishers; and finally, to my wife Ruth for tenaciously encouraging me from the beginning to put my notes and messages into printed form.

Solomon wrote, ". . . of making many books there is no end; and much study is a weariness of the flesh" (Eccl. 12:12). On a sea of books that flood the marketplace, we launch this series of THRU THE BIBLE with the hope that it might draw many to the one Book, *The Bible*.

J. VERNON MCGEE

The
ACTS
of the Apostles

INTRODUCTION

The Book of Acts, sometimes called the fifth Gospel, is a continuation of the Gospel of Luke. Dr. Luke is the writer, as he states in his introduction (v. 1). Sir William Ramsay, after making a critical study of Luke's writings, declared that Luke was the greatest historian, ancient or modern.

The Book of Acts is remarkable in many ways. It is a bridge between the Gospels and the Epistles. The New Testament without the Book of Acts leaves a great yawning gap. As Dr. Houston puts it, "If the book of Acts were gone, there would be nothing to replace it." The last recorded fact about Jesus in the Gospel of Matthew is the Resurrection, which is recorded in Acts 1. In the Gospel of Mark, the last recorded act of Jesus is the Ascension, which is also recorded in Acts 1. In the Gospel of Luke, the last recorded fact is the promise of the Holy Spirit. That is also in Acts 1. And in the Gospel of John the last recorded fact is the second coming of Christ. You guessed it—that is also in Acts 1. It is as if the four Gospels had been poured into a funnel, and they all come down into this jug of the first chapter of the Book of Acts. Also the great missionary commission, which appears in all four Gospels, is confirmed in the Book of Acts.

The Book of Acts furnishes a ladder on which to place the Epistles. It would be an enriching experience to read them together, as Acts gives the history of the founding of the churches to which the Epistles are directed.

The Book of Acts records the beginning of the church, the birth of the church. The book of Genesis records the origin of the spiritual body which we designate as the church.

The theme or key to the Book of Acts is found in 1:8: "But ye shall receive power, after that the Holy Ghost is come upon you: and ye shall be witnesses unto me both in Jerusalem, and in all Judaea, and in Samaria, and unto the uttermost part of the earth."

The book divides naturally according to this key verse. The first seven chapters record the Lord Jesus Christ at work by the Holy Spirit through the apostles in *Jerusalem.* Chapters 8 through 12 record the Lord Jesus Christ at work by the Holy Spirit through the apostles in *Judea* and *Samaria.* The remainder of the book is devoted to the Lord Jesus Christ at work by the Holy Spirit through the apostles unto the *uttermost part of the earth.*

The Book of Acts is not complete. It breaks off with Paul in his own hired house in Rome. It has no proper ending. Do you know why? It is because the Book of Acts is a continuing story. Perhaps the Lord has Dr. Luke up there writing the next chapters now. Perhaps he is recording what you and I do for Christ in the power of the Holy Spirit. I hope so.

Some special features of the Book of Acts are:

1. Prominence of the Lord Jesus Christ. The Lord Jesus has left His disciples now. He is gone. He has ascended in the first chapter of the book. But He is still at work! He has just moved His position, His location. He has moved His headquarters. As long as He was here on this earth, His headquarters were in Capernaum. Now His headquarters are at the right hand of the Father. The Lord Jesus Christ is prominent. He is at work from the vantage place of heaven itself.

2. Prominence of the Holy Spirit. Christ promised to send the Holy Spirit. This promise is mentioned in the Gospel of John four times (John 1:33; 7:37–39; 14:16–17; 20:22). The same promise is given in the Book of Acts (Acts 1:8). You and I are living in the age of the Holy Spirit. The great fact of this age is the indwelling of the Holy Spirit in believers.

3. The power of the church. There is a power in the church and, of course, this is the working of the Spirit of God. That power of the early church is not manifested in churches today. Why? Because the early church operated on a high spiritual level which has not again been attained in any age since then. However, it is the Holy Spirit working through the believer when any service brings honor and glory to the Lord Jesus Christ.

4. Prominence of the church, visible and invisible. The church is a new institution. It has come into existence in the Book of Acts.

5. Prominence of places. The book begins at Jerusalem and ends in Rome. Sir William Ramsay checked all the places mentioned by Dr. Luke and found them to be accurate.

6. Prominence of persons. Dr. Luke mentions 110 persons by name, besides the references to multitudes or crowds. I believe that by the end of the first century there were millions of believers in the world. The church had a phenomenal growth in those first two to three hundred years. It certainly has slowed down today, exactly as our Lord said it would.

7. Prominence of the Resurrection. The Resurrection is the center of gospel preaching. In too many churches today, we have one Easter sermon once a year. As a pastor, many times I have featured Easter in August. People would come just to find out what had happened to the preacher. They thought the heat was getting to me. However, in the early church the resurrection of Jesus Christ was the very center and heart of the message, and no sermon was preached without it. The theme of Peter on the Day of Pentecost was the resurrection of Jesus Christ. He explained that what was taking place on that day was because of the fact that Jesus was now in heaven at the right hand of God and had sent His Holy Spirit into the world. It was all due to the Resurrection. You will find that the Resurrection is the very heart of the messages of Paul.

There are a great many people and preachers who like to "ride a hobby." Some people like to ride the hobby of prophecy; others dwell on the Keswick message or some other facet or phase. Now, if you want to ride a hobby, let me suggest one for you: the resurrection of Jesus Christ. In the early church, every Sunday was Easter, a day to proclaim the Resurrection. "He is risen!" was proclaimed everywhere (see Matt. 27:64).

8. There is a prominence of Peter in the first section of the book and of Paul in the last section. There is a strange omission of the other apostles. God had good reasons, I am sure, for emphasizing the ministry of these two men.

Also there is a human reason. I believe that Dr. Luke was acquainted with the ministries of these two men. He was an associate of Paul. Some people hold the idea that there was a disagreement between Peter and Paul. Very candidly, I am of the opinion that Dr. Luke and Peter and Paul got together a great many times and had many talks.

The proper title for this historical book has always been a problem. The Bible which I use is the authorized version, and there it is called *The Acts of the Apostles*. The Codex Vaticanus and the revised versions also call it *The Acts of the Apostles*. Robert Lee called it *The Acts of the Ascended and Glorified Lord*. The Bantu title is *Words Concerning Deeds*.

I would rather think that the key is given to us in the first two verses of the first chapter. On the basis of this, I would venture a title which is a rather long one: *The Lord Jesus Christ at Work by the Holy Spirit through the Apostles*.

OUTLINE

I. The Lord Jesus Christ at Work by the Holy Spirit through the Apostles in Jerusalem, Chapters 1—7
  A. Preparation for the Coming of the Spirit, Chapter 1
    1. Introduction, Chapter 1:1–2
    2. Forty Days Post-Resurrection Ministry of Jesus, Chapter 1:3–8
    3. Ascension and Promise of the Return of Jesus, Chapter 1:9–11
    4. Waiting for the Spirit, Chapter 1:12–14
    5. Appointment of an Apostle, Chapter 1:15–26
  B. Day of Pentecost
    (Bethlehem of the Holy Spirit), Chapter 2
    1. Coming of the Holy Spirit, Chapter 2:1–13
    2. First Sermon in the Church Age of Peter, Chapter 2:14–47
  C. First Miracle of the Church; Peter's Second Sermon, Chapter 3
    1. Healing of Lame Man, Chapter 3:1–11
    2. Appealing and Revealing Address of Peter, Chapter 3:12–26
    3. Believing Five Thousand Men (Results), Chapter 4:4
  D. First Persecution of the Church; Power of the Holy Spirit, Chapter 4
  E. Death of Ananias and Sapphira; Second Persecution, Chapter 5
  F. Appointment of Deacons; Witness of Stephen, a Deacon, Chapter 6
  G. Stephen's Address and Martyrdom (First Martyr), Chapter 7

II. The Lord Jesus Christ at Work by the Holy Spirit through the Apostles in Judea and Samaria, Chapters 8—12
  A. Conversion of Ethiopian Eunuch (Son of Ham), Chapter 8
  B. Conversion of Saul of Tarsus (Son of Shem), Chapter 9

CHAPTER 15

THEME: The council at Jerusalem

Now that the first missionary journey of Paul and Barnabas has been completed and the churches which they established in the Galatian country are 100 percent gentile, the church faces its first great crisis.

In Judea many of the Hebrew converts are Pharisees who have no intention of giving up the Mosaic system. They assert that the Gentiles must also come into the church through the Mosaic system. In fact, they believe that Gentiles are not saved until they are circumcised.

The news of this contention reaches the church in Jerusalem. The apostles must now face up to the question. What course is the church to take? So in Jerusalem the first church council convenes to resolve the matter.

Down through history you will find that there have been other church councils that have decided other great issues, such as the validity and the inerrancy of the Scriptures. Another council decided upon the deity of Christ and the fact that He is both God and man. And there have been other important councils when differences arose in the church. Some folk may think that we need a council in our day. We certainly do. However, I am afraid there could never been an agreement because too many churches are far removed from the person of Christ. A council that cannot meet around the person of Christ is not actually a church council because the Lord Jesus Christ is the very center of the church. The issue is not one of ritual, or of membership, or of ceremony. The central issue is that of one's personal relationship to Jesus Christ. Unfortunately, people who are personally far removed from Christ and who do not experience fellowship with Him want to argue about ritual. Oh, they may carry a big Bible under their arm, go to church on Sunday and sing the hymns lustily, but on Monday the Lord Jesus is far removed from them.

Friend, the Lord Jesus should occupy the very center of our lives.

We should think of Him constantly. We should not see a sunset without thinking of the One who made it. He should be brought into our daily living, into all situations of life, our tensions and our anxieties.

Now let's turn our attention to this council at Jerusalem. An outstanding group has come together here. These men have convened in order to consider this great issue: law versus grace, or law versus liberty.

THE QUESTION OF CIRCUMCISION

And certain men which came down from Judaea taught the brethren, and said, Except ye be circumcised after the manner of Moses; ye cannot be saved [Acts 15:1].

Here is the crux of the issue. It is not simply a question of whether one should be circumcised or not, whether one should eat meat or not. The question is: Must one do any of these things in order to be saved? Now we will move on and penetrate a little deeper into their problem.

When therefore Paul and Barnabas had no small dissension and disputation with them, they determined that Paul and Barnabas, and certain other of them, should go up to Jerusalem unto the apostles and elders about this question [Acts 15:2].

Again I call attention to Dr. Luke's use of the diminutive. "No small dissension" really means they had a regular donnybrook! It was a heated debate.

We need to realize here that it is really the Gospel which is under question at this council. The Epistle to the Galatians gives us a full explanation of the council.

The word *Gospel* is used in two senses in the New Testament. First of all, there are the *facts* of the Gospel. These are absolutely basic and essential. Paul gives those facts in the first five verses of 1 Corinthians 15. It is the death, the burial, and the resurrection of the Lord Jesus Christ. "Moreover, brethren, I declare unto you the gospel which I preached unto you, which also ye have received, and wherein ye stand; By which also ye are saved, if ye keep in memory what I preached unto you, unless ye have believed in vain. For I delivered unto you first of all that which I also received, how that Christ died for our sins according to the scriptures; And that he was buried, and that he rose again the third day according to the scriptures: and that he was seen of Cephas, then of the twelve." These are the facts of the Gospel, and they concern the person of Christ. I move on down to 1 Corinthians 15:15–17: "Yea, and we are found false witnesses of God; because we have testified of God that he raised up Christ: whom he raised not up, if so be that the dead rise not. For if the dead rise not, then is not Christ raised: And if Christ be not raised, your faith is vain; ye are yet in your sins." Face up to it, my friend; if Christ is not raised from the dead, then there is no Gospel at all. But thanks be to God, ". . . Now is Christ risen from the dead, and become the firstfruits of them that slept" (1 Cor. 15:20). The facts of the Gospel are the death, burial, and resurrection of Christ.

The second sense of the word *Gospel* is the *interpretation* of the facts. It is this interpretation which is the basic truth in the Epistle to the Galatians. That is the crux of the whole matter at this first council at Jerusalem. Thus the Gospel also hinges on this fact which Paul states in Galatians 3:22: "But the scripture hath concluded all under sin, that the promise by faith of Jesus Christ might be given to them that believe." What must one do to be saved? Nothing more nor less than *believe*. Again in Galatians 2:15–16: "We who are Jews by nature, and not sinners of the Gentiles, Knowing that a man is not justified by the works of the law, but by the faith of Jesus Christ, even we have believed in Jesus Christ, that we might be justified by the faith of Christ, and not by the works of the law: for by the works of the law shall no flesh be justified." That is important to see.

The Judaizers of that day were different from the liberals of today. The liberal will actually deny the facts of the Gospel. He will deny the physical resurrection of Christ. Some go so far as to say that Jesus Christ is just a myth, that He never lived or died. Most of them do not try to upset history quite to that extent. However, they deny that Jesus died *for our sins.*

In the first century the Judaizers did not deny the facts of the Gospel—there simply were too many witnesses. Paul says that over five hundred people saw the risen Christ at one time. My friend, if you get five hundred witnesses into any law court, you will win your case! Also the apostles were witnesses to the risen Christ. They were there to testify to it. The facts of the Gospel were not under question by the Judaizers.

The contention arose over the *interpretation* of those facts. What did Christ do for you on the cross? Is the work of Christ adequate to save you? Do you need to go through some ritual or something else in order to be saved? Must you go through the Law? These are the questions they were asking.

Now let's return to Acts 15 and go with Paul and Barnabas up to Jerusalem.

And being brought on their way by the church, they passed through Phenice and Samaria, declaring the conversion of the Gentiles: and they caused great joy unto all the brethren.

And when they were come to Jerusalem, they were received of the church, and of the apostles and elders, and they declared all things that God had done with them [Acts 15:3–4].

Paul and Barnabas give a report to the church in Jerusalem just as they had done to the church in Antioch. They tell them, "We have preached the Gospel, and men and women over in the Galatian country have trusted Christ. They know nothing about Mosaic Law. They trusted Christ and were saved."

But there rose up certain of the sect of the Pharisees which believed, saying, That it was needful to circumcise them, and to command them to keep the law of Moses [Acts 15:5].

They wanted to add something to the Gospel. Friend, whenever you add something to the Gospel, you no longer have the Gospel but you have a religion. You no longer have the Gospel of Jesus Christ. The only approach that you can make to Jesus Christ is by faith. We must all come to Him by faith. He won't let us come any other way. Jesus said, ". . . I am the way, the truth, and the life: no man cometh unto the Father, but by me" (John 14:6). He's bottled the whole world into this. There is only one question God asks the lost world: "What do you do with My Son who died for you?" God doesn't give us some little Sunday School lesson by saying, "I want you to be a good boy. I want you to join a church. I want you go to through this and that ritual." That kind of teaching is only for an insipid *religion*. It does not come from God. God is saying, "My Son died for you. What will you do with Him?" The answer to that question will determine your eternal destiny. This is the issue being discussed at the council in Jerusalem. This is really exciting.

> **And the apostles and elders came together for to consider of this matter [Acts 15:6].**

THE DECISION OF THE COUNCIL

The apostles and elders had come together to argue this thing out. The disputes were hot and heavy. A decision must be made, and Simon Peter is the first one to express his decision.

> **And when there had been much disputing, Peter rose up, and said unto them, Men and brethren, ye know how that a good while ago God made choice among us, that the Gentiles by my mouth should hear the word of the gospel, and believe [Acts 15:7].**

I don't think that this is the first time Peter spoke. If he had been quiet through all that time of disputing, it certainly would not have been consistent with his character. No, I'm of the opinion that he had already put in his two bits worth before this. But now he is going to sum up the whole thing. This is not a new decision for Peter. Peter had already declared this same thing at the time of the conversion of Cornelius. Remember that Peter himself had been shocked by the truth of it. He was told to go into the home of a Gentile and preach the Gospel without the Law. The people were uncircumcised, they didn't follow the Mosaic system, they ate pork—and yet they were saved!

The council would listen to Simon Peter because he was narrow-minded—I don't say this in an ugly way—I mean that he was a Jew of the Jews. He himself said he had never eaten anything unclean, and he wouldn't have thought of entering the home of a Gentile. He stuck as close to the Mosaic system as any man could. So if Peter spoke up, they would listen.

Now he testifies that the Gentiles had heard the Gospel from his mouth and had believed. You mean they were actually saved? Yes, they were saved by grace. Peter himself had to learn that salvation is not decided by whether one eats meat or doesn't eat meat, whether one eats pork or doesn't eat pork. Salvation is not dependent on our observation of the Sabbath, or Sunday, or any other day. Salvation is by grace through faith. We are free to choose what we wish to do about these other things. We have freedom in that connection.

> **And God, which knoweth the hearts, bare them witness, giving them the Holy Ghost, even as he did unto us;**
>
> **And put no difference between us and them, purifying their hearts by faith [Acts 15:8–9].**

Does Peter say that God purified their hearts by keeping the Law? No! By going through a ceremony? No! By joining a church? No! By *faith*. Peter said, "I went into the home of Cornelius. I gave them the facts of the Gospel. They believed and were saved—the Holy Ghost came upon them just as He had come to us in Jerusalem."

My friend, this is always the only way of salvation. It is by faith. You don't have to do anything to merit your salvation. Jesus Christ did it all for you nineteen hundred years ago. All God asks you to do is to accept His Son who died for you.

Now therefore why tempt ye God, to put a yoke upon the neck of the disciples, which neither our fathers nor we were able to bear? [Acts 15:10].

Simon Peter makes a tremendous admission here. He says that neither they nor their fathers kept the Law. I have said this many times before, and I will say it many, many times more: God has never saved anybody through the keeping of the Law. Do you know why? There has never been a person who has kept it. God saves on one basis and one basis only: faith in the death and resurrection of the Lord Jesus Christ.

Before the time of Christ, men brought a sacrifice to God. They brought that sacrifice by faith. Abel understood that the little lamb could never take away sin. He understood that the little lamb pointed to the One about whom God had told his mother. He had said that the Seed of the woman would come and would bruise the head of the serpent (Gen. 3:15). Abel believed that. He believed God. He was saved by faith.

So Simon Peter says, "To tell the truth—why don't we admit it—we can't keep the Law." You see, there is nothing more hypocritical than to pretend that you are living life on a high spiritual plane, that you are living by the Sermon on the Mount and you are keeping God's Law. There is no use pretending.

I wish I could look you in the eye and ask you, "Why don't you admit that you are a lost sinner? Why don't you confess that you do not please God, that you have no capacity for Him? Why don't you come to God as a sinner and trust Christ as your Savior?" He will receive you! ". . . Him that cometh to me I will in no wise cast out" (John 6:37). That is the way I came to the Lord. Everybody I have ever met who has been saved has come to Him in that way. Saul of Tarsus came like that. The Ethiopian eunuch came like that. All who have come to Christ have come like that.

But we believe that through the grace of the Lord Jesus Christ we shall be saved, even as they [Acts 15:11].

Simon Peter puts it so nicely. The Jews must be saved in exactly the same way that the Gentiles are saved. I'm pretty sure that Simon Peter still didn't eat pork at this time, but he implies, "I'm not saved because I don't eat pork; I'm saved because I have trusted Christ." He is saved by the grace of God.

> **Then all the multitude kept silence, and gave audience to Barnabas and Paul, declaring what miracles and wonders God had wrought among the Gentiles by them [Acts 15:12].**

What a story they had to tell! I wish I could have sat in on the council of Jerusalem. Especially I wish I could have heard these two men tell their experiences in the Galatian country.

The next man to get up to speak will be James. I want to stop here for a moment to explain that this was not James, the brother of John, as he had already died a martyr's death (Acts 12:2). There is some question as to who this James was. We know that he became the leader of the church in Jerusalem. He has already been mentioned as a leader by Peter in Acts 12:17. This may have been James, the son of Alphaeus, one of the twelve (Matt. 10:3). However, the tradition of the church from the early church fathers has identified this man as James, the half brother of our Lord (Matt. 13:55), the same one who wrote the Epistle of James.

I should stop here to make another remark. I believe that the proper way to study the Book of Acts is to study it along with the Epistles. For example, we have already mentioned the Epistle to the Galatians, and during the study of Acts 13 and 14 would be a good time to read that Epistle. At this point in Acts 15 it would be appropriate to study the Epistle of James.

James is going to sum up the thinking of this council at Jerusalem, and He will put down God's program for the future.

We need to remember that these men stood with their noses pressed right up to the window of the opening of a new dispensation. The church had been brought into existence at Penetcost; it was still very new, in its infancy. Some people still do not understand that we live in the age of grace, the period of the church. So let us not be too critical of these men who stood on the threshold of this new age.

And after they had held their peace, James answered, saying, Men and brethren, hearken unto me [Acts 15:13].

I take it that after Simon Peter spoke and after Paul and Barnabas gave their report, there was silence because no one had anything to say. Even the Judaizers were silenced by the reports of what had taken place.

When James speaks to the crowd on that day, he asks them to "hearken," that is, to really listen. What he has to say is very important. So he means that you and I should listen to him, too. Probably all of us should spend more time listening to God and less time doing the talking. Well, now let's listen.

Simeon hath declared how God at the first did visit the Gentiles, to take out of them a people for his name [Acts 15:14].

James completely agrees with Peter. They state the plan of God for today. Is God saving the whole world? No. Is God bringing in His kingdom? No. Then what is God doing today? He is visiting the Gentiles to take out of them a people for His name. We learn in Revelation that standing before the throne of God there will be those of every tribe and tongue and people and nation. The Word of God is to go out into the world. There will be opposition to it and there will be apostasy, but the Word of God is to go out to all the world because God is calling out a people for His name.

This is why I am so anxious to get out the Word of God. Right now there are people of every color, every clime, every condition, every race, and practically every nation who hear Bible teaching by radio. We broadcast on stations that pretty well circle the globe. Thank God we can use this means to get out the Word of God. What does God do with that Word? He is calling out a people for His name. Not everyone who hear believes the Word. Not everyone accepts the good news of Jesus Christ. But of those who hear, God calls out a people for His name. Underline verse 14 in your Bible—I have it circled in mine. God

is visiting the Gentiles to take out of them a people for His name. I am
so thankful that He has given me the opportunity to tell people about
salvation in the Lord Jesus Christ and to teach them the Word of God.

> **And to this agree the words of the prophets; as it is writ-
> ten [Acts 15:15].**

Do you think this new age is contrary to the teaching of the Old Testament? Well, it is not. The words of the prophets agree to this.

Now James begins to quote a prophet (see Amos 9:11–12). "After
this," which in the prophet is "in that day." What does it mean? After
what? After God has called out a people for His name. God today is
calling out individuals for His name. They become a part of the
church, the body of believers. The day is coming when God will remove His church from this world—this we call the Rapture. It is the
next event on the agenda of God. After this—after His church has left
the earth—

> **After this I will return, and will build again the taber-
> nacle of David, which is fallen down and I will build
> again the ruins thereof, and I will set it up [Acts 15:16].**

The tabernacle of David is fallen down—there's no doubt about that.
There is no one around from the line of David. The only One who has
that claim is sitting at the right hand of God at this very moment. But
God is going to build it again. He is going to send Jesus back. God says
to His Son: "But to which of the angels said he at any time, Sit on my
right hand, until I make thine enemies thy footstool?" (Heb. 1:13).
God is bringing all the enemies of Christ to be put under His feet. The
rebellion is going to be over one of these days. Until the day when He
sends Jesus back, the Spirit of God is saying, "Kiss the Son, lest he be
angry, and ye perish from the way, when his wrath is kindled but a
little. Blessed are all they that put their trust in him" (Ps. 2:12).

The program of God is clearly outlined. He is calling a people out
of the world now. His second step with the world will be to build again

the line of David. That is, he will reestablish the Davidic rule over Israel.

> **That the residue of men might seek after the Lord, and all the Gentiles, upon whom my name is called, saith the Lord, who doeth all these things [Acts 15:17].**

Today he is calling a people out of the Gentiles. However, in that day there will be a great turning to God. This will be after the church has left this world. These are the ones who will enter the kingdom. The "residue of men might seek after the Lord" and "all the Gentiles, upon whom my name is called" will turn to the Lord. This, then, will be the third step in God's program.

> **Known unto God are all his works from the beginning of the world [Acts 15:18].**

James has been doing the summing up. He understands that there is a definite program which God is following. Now James is ready to hand down his decision, and it is a very important decision.

> **Wherefore my sentence is, that we trouble not them, which from among the Gentiles are turned to God:**
>
> **But that we write unto them, that they abstain from pollutions of idols and from fornication, and from things strangled, and from blood [Acts 15:19–20].**

The decision is that Gentiles who have turned to God are not to be put under the Mosaic system. However, they are going to ask the Gentiles to do certain things out of courtesy. They will ask them to abstain from pollutions of idols. The reason this is so specifically mentioned will come up again in 1 Corinthians in the section about eating meat. The situation was that the gentile world of that day worshipped idols, and in a city like Corinth, for example, the people would take their best animals and offer them to their pagan gods. They were very clever about this. They would take the animal in and make an offering of it, and the gods, which were "spiritual," ate the "spiritual" animal. Then the people would take the meat and sell it in the meat markets at the heathen temples. That was the place to buy the best steaks in that day—the filet mignon and the porterhouse and New York cuts.

The Gentiles were not offended by this. They had always bought their meat at these markets, and it was not a matter of conscience for them. However, for the Israelite Christian this would be very offensive. They had been brought up and trained not to eat anything that had been offered to an idol. So the thought here is that the Gentile who invites a Jewish brother over for dinner should not offend him by serving him something that had been offered to idols. So this request was not a matter of putting the Gentiles under Mosaic Law. It was a request that they should not to do something which would be very offensive to their Jewish brothers.

They were also requested to abstain from fornication. Again, we need to understand the background to see why this is specifically mentioned. Adultery was so common among the Gentiles in that day that the conscience had been dulled. In fact, adultery was actually part of the religious rite. The Gentiles who had become Christians were to "abstain from fornication."

In America we are going back to paganism today. Folk talk about a new morality. Friend, what they call new morality is old paganism. Our ancestors came out of the forest half naked, eating raw meat, and indulging in gross immorality. There is nothing new about the "new" morality!

Also, the Jerusalem council asked the gentile Christians to abstain from things strangled and from blood, which would be very offensive to their Jewish brothers. This again was a matter of courtesy.

For Moses of old time hath in every city them that preach him, being read in the synagogues every sabbath day [Acts 15:21].

I think we should review what James has said. He fits the church into the program of the prophets although the church is not a subject of prophecy. God is taking out of the Gentiles a people for His name to-day. Then the program of the prophets will follow.

1. "After this" means after the church is taken out of the world. "I will return" (v. 16) is the second coming of Christ described in Revelation 19.

2. He "will build again the ruins" of the house of David that today has fallen down (v. 16).

3. When Christ returns, there will be a way for the remainder of men to "seek after the Lord" (v. 17).

4. Then *all* the Gentiles will be in the kingdom "in that day" (Amos 9:11).

The important contrast is between "out of them (Gentiles)" (v. 14) and "all the Gentiles" (v. 17).

THE DECISION OF THE COUNCIL IS ANNOUNCED

Then pleased it the apostles and elders, with the whole church, to send chosen men of their own company to Antioch with Paul and Barnabas; namely, Judas surnamed Barsabas, and Silas, chief men among the brethren:

And they wrote letters by them after this manner; The apostles and elders and brethren send greeting unto the brethren which are of the Gentiles in Antioch and Syria and Cilicia [Acts 15:22-23].

There are some new men mentioned here. Silas will be the partner of Paul on the next journey. Notice the love that is demonstrated in this letter. They wrote to the Gentiles who had turned to God and they called them "the brethren which are of the Gentiles."

Forasmuch as we have heard, that certain which went out from us have troubled you with words, subverting your souls, saying, Ye must be circumcised, and keep the law: to whom we gave no such commandment [Acts 15:24].

These people who had gone out, the Judaizers, had no authority from the church in Jerusalem. In fact, we can say that anyone who tries to put a believer under the Law today is not doing it on the authority of the Word of God.

> **It seemed good unto us, being assembled with one accord, to send chosen men unto you with our beloved Barnabas and Paul [Acts 15:25].**

Isn't this a lovely expression?

> **Men that have hazarded their lives for the name of our Lord Jesus Christ [Acts 15:26].**

The church sends out men who have been tested, men who have hazarded their lives. Friend, how much have you suffered for Him? What has it cost you? Have you paid a price in order to get out the Word of God?

> **We have sent therefore Judas and Silas, who shall also tell you the same things by mouth [Acts 15:27].**

You can see that if they had sent only Barnabas and Paul the people might have said, "Well, of course, these two men would bring back that kind of a report." So they send along Judas and Silas in order to confirm the fact that this was the decision of the council.

> **For it seemed good to the Holy Ghost, and to us, to lay upon you no greater burden than these necessary things [Acts 15:28].**

"It seemed good to the Holy Ghost, and to us"—the Holy Spirit was guiding and directing them in this decision.

> **That ye abstain from meats offered to idols, and from blood, and from things strangled, and from fornication:**

**from which if ye keep yourselves, ye shall do well. Fare
ye well [Acts 15:29].**

That is the report. That is all they have to say to them. Gentile believers
are not required to meet any of the demands of the Mosaic system, but
they are to exercise courtesy to those who do—especially in the area of
meats offered to idols, and of course they are not to commit fornication.

**So when they were dismissed, they came to Antioch:
and when they had gathered the multitude together, they
delivered the epistle:**

**Which when they had read, they rejoiced for the conso-
lation [Acts 15:30–31].**

There is consolation and comfort in the Gospel; there is nothing but
condemnation in the Law. The Law condemns. The Law is a mirror.
When I look in it, I say, "Oh, McGee, you are ugly! You have fallen
short of the glory of God." But the Gospel says, "Come on to God. He
wants to receive you. He will save you by His grace." It is a comfort,
you see.

**And Judas and Silas, being prophets also themselves,
exhorted the brethren with many words, and confirmed
them.**

**And after they had tarried there a space, they were let go
in peace from the brethren unto the apostles.**

**Notwithstanding it pleased Silas to abide there still
[Acts 15:32–34].**

It is evident that Paul and Silas got along well together. Silas must have
liked Paul and enjoyed working with him. So he stayed there at the
church in Antioch. He must have been excited about working with
these gentile believers. At any rate, he stayed.

Paul also and Barnabas continued in Antioch, teaching and preaching the word of the Lord, with many others also [Acts 15:35].

Paul and Barnabas were actually the pastors of the church there.

PLANS FOR A SECOND MISSIONARY JOURNEY

And some days after Paul said unto Barnabas, Let us go again and visit our brethren in every city where we have preached the word of the Lord, and see how they do [Acts 15:36].

Paul had a concern for the churches, a genuine concern for the believers. Knowing how fickle the Galatians were, he thought it would be a good idea to go back again and to visit those churches.

And Barnabas determined to take with them John, whose surname was Mark [Acts 15:37].

We know Barnabas as a very generous, gracious fellow. He is eager to give John Mark another chance. But I want to note that when he has made up his mind, he is hardheaded. Remember that both these men were human. Paul and Barnabas each took a stand and would not budge.

But Paul thought not good to take him with them, who departed from them from Pamphylia, and went not with them to the work [Acts 15:38].

Paul had his convictions also. Barnabas wants to take John Mark along, and Paul will not do it. Well, I'm glad these two brethren had this little altercation because it teaches me that these men were human and that even the saints can disagree without being disagreeable. They didn't break up anything. They did not split the church and form two different churches in Antioch. They just disagreed. It's all right to disagree with some of the brethren.

> **And the contention was so sharp between them, that they departed asunder one from the other: and so Barnabas took Mark, and sailed unto Cyprus [Acts 15:39].**

The account does not follow Barnabas any longer. He went to Cyprus and there he had a great ministry. Barnabas had come from Cyprus; it was his home. He had a desire to take the Gospel to his own people. We know from tradition that he had a great ministry there, and from Cyprus a great ministry was carried on in North Africa.

At this point Barnabas sails off the pages of the Scriptures. The Bible does not give us information about his ministry. From here on we are going to follow Paul.

> **And Paul chose Silas, and departed, being recommended by the brethren unto the grace of God.**

> **And he went through Syria and Cilicia, confirming the churches [Acts 15:40–41].**

The church now has two great mission projects where before they had only one. Barnabas is going in one direction and Paul is going another. This is God's method. God will use both these men. Paul now has Silas with him, and the brethren recommended them "unto the grace of God."

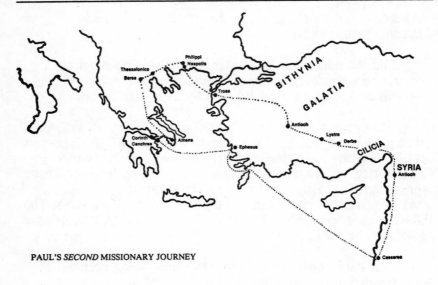

PAUL'S *SECOND* MISSIONARY JOURNEY

CHAPTER 16

THEME: The second missionary journey of Paul

The final verse of chapter 15 actually told of the beginning of the journey. Paul and Silas "went through Syria and Cilicia, confirming the churches." From there *they* will go up into the Galatian country. *Paul* will visit the Galatian churches because that is where the problem had arisen with the Judaizers. The epistle to the Galatians is Paul's letter to them, sternly warning them about being led astray by those who are trying to put them under the Mosaic system. It is his strongest declaration and defense of the doctrine of justification by faith. Not only is a sinner saved by grace through faith, but the saved sinner lives by grace. Grace is a way *to* life and a way *of* life.

Again let me suggest that you follow Paul's journey on the map. You will find that traveling with Paul is a very thrilling experience. On this second missionary journey we will go with him to Europe (after he has received the vision of the man in Macedonia). We will see that he arrives in Philippi where he ends up in the local jail. At midnight Paul and Silas pray and sing praises! An earthquake shakes the jail, the doors are opened, and the jailer opens his heart to receive Christ as Savior.

PAUL REVISITS THE CHURCHES OF GALATIA

Then came he to Derbe and Lystra: and, behold, a certain disciple was there, named Timotheus, the son of a certain woman, which was a Jewess, and believed; but his father was a Greek:

Which was well reported of by the brethren that were at Lystra and Iconium [Acts 16:1–2].

Paul first comes to Derbe, then over to Lystra where he finds this young man Timotheus. Paul knew his mother and his grandmother, and he had turned this young man to the Lord on his first trip. So Paul takes him with him. The team is now Paul, Silas, and Timothy.

> **Him would Paul have to go forth with him; and took and circumcised him because of the Jews which were in those quarters: for they knew all that his father was a Greek [Acts 16:3].**

I want to note carefully the method of the apostle Paul. When he went up to Jerusalem, he took along Titus, a Gentile, who wasn't circumcised—and Paul wasn't about to have him circumcised. However, now Paul wants to take along Timothy as a fellow missionary. He wants Timothy to go out to reach people for Christ. Since he doesn't want any kind of argument or any reason for offense, he has Timothy circumcised. This is not because there is any merit in circumcision, but because he doesn't want it to be an issue. This is what Paul wrote in 1 Corinthians 9:19–20: "For though I be free from all men, yet have I made myself servant unto all, that I might gain the more. And unto the Jews I became as a Jew, that I might gain the Jews; to them that are under the law, as under the law, that I might gain them that are under the law." Paul did this in order to break down all arguments.

Sometimes people come to me and say they want to join a certain church but that church has a different idea of baptism than they hold. They ask if they should be baptized and join the church anyway. So I ask them, "Is the church a good Bible-teaching church? Does it teach salvation only and alone through faith in the Lord Jesus Christ? Is it a place where you can serve, and be blessed, and grow in grace and in the knowledge of the truth?" If they can answer yes to these questions, then I tell them to go ahead and be baptized and affiliate with that church. There are fundamentals of faith in which there can be no deviation. However, there are forms and rituals which are not essential to salvation, and I believe there is a great deal of elasticity in these areas. This was Paul's feeling. Certainly circumcision had no bearing on Timothy's salvation, but the rite was performed so that the ministry of Timothy with the Jews would not be handicapped.

And as they went through the cities, they delivered them the decrees for to keep, that were ordained of the apostles and elders which were at Jerusalem.

And so were the churches established in the faith, and increased in number daily [Acts 16:4–5].

Paul has another tremendous ministry in Galatia. Not only does he visit the churches which had been founded the first time, but multitudes in other places turn to Christ. New churches are formed and there is an increase in number daily.

PAUL GOES TO PHILIPPI

Now when they had gone throughout Phrygia and the region of Galatia, and were forbidden of the Holy Ghost to preach the word in Asia [Acts 16:6].

Galatia includes all this area. I am of the opinion that Paul moved into the northern part of the country at this particular point. The province of Asia is down south where Ephesus is. In fact, Ephesus was the chief city of the province of Asia. Paul may have been planning to make a circuit through Asia Minor. This was a heavily populated area in that day, and it was really the center of Greek culture. This was a great commercial area, a great political area, a great educational area. Paul would make a great circle by going through the Galatian country, then Phrygia, then south into the province of Asia, and then back again to Antioch to report to the home church.

The Spirit of God had something else in mind. We are told that the Holy Spirit forbade him to preach the Word down in Asia. That is really amazing, isn't it? Paul wanted to go there, and the Spirit of God wanted the Word of God given out, but the Spirit of God wanted Paul in a different place at this time. So Paul naturally thought that if he could not go south, he would go north. Bithynia was in the north, along the Black Sea. That also was a large population center, and there was a very heavy concentration of Hebrews in that area. This section is in Turkey today.

> After they were come to Mysia, they assayed to go into
> Bithynia: but the Spirit suffered them not [Acts 16:7].

The Spirit forbade them to go south into the province of Asia. Then the Spirit of God forbade them to go north into Bithynia. He has come from the east. Where will he go? Well, there is only one direction left and that is west. You see, it was not Horace Greeley of *The New York Sun* who first said, "Go west, young man, go west." Instead it was the Spirit of God speaking to the apostle Paul!

So Paul kept going west until he came to Troas. He had to stop there because from that point he would need a ship to continue. Paul couldn't imagine what he was to do or where he was to go from that point.

> And they passing by Mysia came down to Troas [Acts
> 16:8].

I think that if we had met Paul during the time of his delay in Troas, we could have asked him, "Paul, where are you going?" I'm sure his reply would have been, "I don't know." I'm afraid our next statement would have been something like this: "Now brother Paul, do you mean that the great Apostle of the Gentiles doesn't know where he is going next? Surely you must know the will of God for your life." Then we would have sat down for a nice long lecture on how to determine the will of God in his life. My, I've read so many books on that subject—it's too bad Paul didn't have one of those books with him at that time! Paul does not know the will of God. Why? Because the *Spirit of God* is leading him. Paul is simply waiting. It is going to take a mighty movement to get Paul out of Asia and move him over into Europe.

> And a vision appeared to Paul in the night; There stood
> a man of Macedonia, and prayed him, saying, Come
> over into Macedonia, and help us [Acts 16:9].

This is Paul's call into Macedonia. Now Macedonia is across the Aegean Sea, over in Europe. Paul is in Asia. The Gospel is going to cross from Asia into Europe. The Spirit of God is moving him in that direction.

I do not know why Paul was not moved east to China. All I know is that the Spirit of God moved him west to Europe. I thank God that this is the direction he went. At that particular time my ancestors, from one side of the family, were roaming in the forests of Germany. They were pagan and they were evil, worshipping all kinds of idols. They were a low, heathen people. The other side of my family came from Scotland, and perhaps my ancestors were already in Scotland at that time or came there a little later. At any rate, I am told they were the dirtiest, filthiest savages that have ever been on the topside of this earth. I thank God the Gospel went to Europe to reach my people over there.

Now maybe you are smiling, thinking that your ancestors were very superior to mine. Well, you can wipe that smile off your face because your ancestors probably were living in the cave right next door to mine! They were just as dirty and just as filthy as mine were. Thank God the Gospel crossed over into Europe. This was a great and significant crossing.

> **And after he had seen the vision, immediately we endeavoured to go into Macedonia, assuredly gathering that the Lord had called us for to preach the gospel unto them [Acts 16:10].**

Note it says "we endeavored to go." We have never had "we" before. It has always been "they" or "them" or "he" or "him." What about "we"? Well, Dr. Luke has now joined the party. It is really quite a party now—in fact, it is a quartet. There may have been others along also, but we have four who are named: Paul, Silas, Timothy, and Dr. Luke. This is quite a delegation that crossed over into Europe.

> **Therefore loosing from Troas, we came with a straight course to Samothracia, and the next day to Neapolis [Acts 16:11].**

Neapolis is just a little inland from the coast.

> **And from thence to Philippi, which is the chief city of
> that part of Macedonia, and a colony: and we were in
> that city abiding certain days [Acts 16:12].**

Philippi was a colony in Macedonia, which means it was a Roman
colony. This would be where the Roman governor resided. These people had Roman customs and they spoke Latin. It would be a city where
they would "do as the Romans do."

This is their first destination in Europe. Paul went to a strategic
center to begin his ministry in Europe. That alone makes the church in
Philippi a remarkable church. For other reasons, which we will learn
when we get to the Epistle to the Philippians, we will see that this
church was close to the heart of Paul. This was the church which loved
him; and Paul loved this church. There were wonderful saints in this
church, as we shall see.

PAUL'S MINISTRY IN PHILIPPI

> **And on the sabbath we went out of the city by a river
> side, where prayer was wont to be made; and we sat
> down, and spake unto the women which resorted
> thither [Acts 16:13].**

Just outside the city, down by the river, there was a prayer meeting. I
wonder whether that prayer meeting had anything to do with Paul
coming over to Europe and the vision of the man of Macedonia! We
will find that the "man of Macedonia" is a woman by the name of
Lydia who was holding this prayer meeting.

> **And a certain woman named Lydia, a seller of purple,
> of the city of Thyatira, which worshipped God, heard
> us: whose heart the Lord opened, that she attended unto
> the things which were spoken of Paul [Acts 16:14].**

Thyatira is over in Asia Minor. It is the place where one of the seven churches was located which received admonition from our Lord in the second chapter of the Book of Revelation. This woman had come from over there. She worshipped the living and true God, but she had very little knowledge.

Lydia was a remarkable person. She was a dominant person and a leader. Apparently she was the leader of the prayer meeting. She will be the first convert to Christ in Europe.

> **And when she was baptized, and her household, she besought us, saying, If ye have judged me to be faithful to the Lord, come into my house, and abide there. And she constrained us [Acts 16:15].**

We do not know anything about Mr. Lydia, but he must have been around there somewhere. There are families like that, you know, where the woman is the dominant one in the family. Apparently that was the way it was in the family of Lydia. Thank God she was that kind of woman because her entire household turned to God through her witness. And now we find Paul and his group staying at her home and boarding there. I would assume she was a person of means and was able to take care of them.

> **And it came to pass, as we went to prayer, a certain damsel possessed with a spirit of divination met us, which brought her masters much gain by soothsaying [Acts 16:16].**

Don't think this was just foolish superstition. This girl was possessed by a demon. We are seeing a resurgence of demonism in our own day. I have before me now a letter from a Christian woman in El Paso, Texas. She got tied up in spiritism by just fooling around with it, not thinking that it was dangerous. She has quite a story. It was hearing the Word of God through our radio program that delivered her from it. She cried out to God, and He delivered her. Demonism is a reality. This girl in Paul's day was demon possessed. She was a slave girl and her masters were using her to make a big profit. The Mafia had already begun in those days.

> **The same followed Paul and us, and cried, saying, These men are the servants of the most high God, which shew unto us the way of salvation.**

> **And this did she many days. But Paul, being grieved, turned and said to the spirit, I command thee in the name of Jesus Christ to come out of her. And he came out the same hour.**

> **And when her masters saw that the hope of their gains was gone, they caught Paul and Silas, and drew them into the marketplace unto the rulers [Acts 16:17–19].**

Paul was able to cast out the demon in the name of the Lord Jesus Christ. This dried up the profit her masters were making, and you know that if you touch a man's pocketbook, he will begin to move. So now these men really turn against Paul and his group.

> **And brought them to the magistrates, saying, These men, being Jews, do exceedingly trouble our city.**

> **And teach customs, which are not lawful for us to receive, neither to observe, being Romans [Acts 16:20–21].**

Remember that Philippi was a Roman colony and practiced Roman idolatry. Paul and his men were charged with trying to change things. Of course the real issue was that the girl's masters had lost their source of income.

> **And the multitude rose up together against them: and the magistrates rent off their clothes, and commanded to beat them.**

> And when they had laid many stripes upon them, they cast them into prison, charging the jailer to keep them safely:
>
> Who, having received such a charge, thrust them into the inner prison, and made their feet fast in the stocks [Acts 16:22–24].

These men are beaten, their backs are lacerated, and they are locked into the stocks.

> And at midnight Paul and Silas prayed, and sang praises unto God: and the prisoners heard them [Acts 16:25].

What a wonderful thing it is that these men were singing praises unto God while they were in such a miserable situation. No wonder the doors were shaken loose!

> And suddenly there was a great earthquake, so that the foundations of the prison were shaken: and immediately all the doors were opened, and every one's bands were loosed.
>
> And the keeper of the prison awaking out of his sleep, and seeing the prison doors open, he drew out his sword, and would have killed himself, supposing that the prisoners had been fled [Acts 16:26–27].

Let's look at this Philippian jailer for a moment. He was responsible for those prisoners. He naturally assumed that if the doors were open and the chains lying loose, the prisoners would be gone. He would be responsible for their escape and would have to forfeit his own life. So he stands there, poised, ready to fall on his own sword. When a man is in a position like that, he thinks about eternity. This man did just that, as his question to Paul indicates.

> But Paul cried with a loud voice, saying, Do thyself no
> harm: for we are all here.
>
> Then he called for a light, and sprang in, and came
> trembling, and fell down before Paul and Silas,
>
> And brought them out, and said, Sirs, what must I do to
> be saved? [Acts 16:28–30].

He had looked into eternity. He knew that he was a lost man.

> And they said, Believe on the Lord Jesus Christ, and
> thou shalt be saved, and thy house [Acts 16:31].

How can a man be saved? By believing on the Lord Jesus Christ. Could
he believe for someone else? No. Believe on the Lord Jesus Christ and
thou shalt be saved, and if thy household believes on the Lord Jesus
Christ, they shall be saved also. That is the meaning here.

> And they spake unto him the word of the Lord, and to all
> that were in his house.
>
> And he took them the same hour of the night, and
> washed their stripes; and was baptized, he and all his,
> straightway [Acts 16:32–33].

What a difference! He had put the stripes on these men. Now he
washes their stripes. He is a changed man.

> And when he had brought them into his house, he set
> meat before them, and rejoiced, believing in God with
> all his house [Acts 16:34].

All in one night they were flogged, thrown into jail, freed by the direct
intervention of God, and now they are being royally entertained in the
home of these rejoicing young converts!

> And when it was day, the magistrates sent the sergeants, saying, Let those men go.
>
> And the keeper of the prison told this saying to Paul, The magistrates have sent to let you go: now therefore depart, and go in peace [Acts 16:35–36].

You see, they realize that what they had done was illegal. Now they are issuing orders to free the prisoners and get them out of town. However, Paul objects. He says that he will not leave under such circumstances.

> But Paul said unto them, They have beaten us openly uncondemned, being Romans, and have cast us into prison; and now do they thrust us out privily? nay verily; but let them come themselves and fetch us out [Acts 16:37].

Of course Paul's reason for insisting upon a public recognition of their innocence was to protect the new believers whom he would soon be leaving there in Philippi.

> And the sergeants told these words unto the magistrates: and they feared, when they heard that they were Romans.
>
> And they came and besought them, and brought them out, and desired them to depart out of the city.
>
> And they went out of the prison, and entered into the house of Lydia: and when they had seen the brethren, they comforted them, and departed [Acts 16:38–40].

CHAPTER 17

THEME: *The second missionary journey of Paul continued (Paul in Thessalonica, Berea, and Athens)*

REMARKS

In this chapter we continue with Paul on his second missionary journey. In chapter 16 we were with him when he crossed over into Europe, a memorable, significant, revolutionary crossing. It brought the Gospel to the ancestors of many of us, who were by no means a superior people. Actually, God chooses the weak things of this world just to let the world know that it is all because of His sovereign grace and not because of merit. We thank Him for sending the Gospel over into Europe.

We went with Paul first to Philippi where he received some rough treatment. Yet, a little church came into existence in that town. When we study the Epistle to that church, we will find that it was closer to the apostle Paul than any other church or any other group of believers.

Now he continues on his journey. I hope you will follow this on the map. You will notice that he goes to Thessalonica and Berea, still traveling westward into Macedonia, then south to Athens. Thessalonica will be his next significant stop for missionary activity.

PAUL'S MINISTRY IN THESSALONICA

Now when they had passed through Amphipolis and Apollonia, they came to Thessalonica, where was a synagogue of the Jews [Acts 17:1].

As we have noted before, Paul used the synagogue as a springboard to get into a city or a community. This would lead him to the devout Jews of the city, and some of those Jews would believe. Never did all of them believe, but some of them did. In fact, most of them would reject him, and this would push him right out to the Gentiles. Then some of the

Gentiles believed. This is how a church would come into existence, a local church composed of Jews and Gentiles.

Amphipolis was also called "Nine Ways," which suggests its importance both strategically and commercially. Most cities are built on the pattern of a square, but this was like a roundhouse, and the wall around it was round. It was an important station on the Via Egnatia, a Roman road which was the prominent thoroughfare through that area. It was five hundred miles from the Hellespont to Dyrrhachium on the Adriatic by this road. This would be the highway which the Roman army would use. This was the route the traders would travel. And now here come some missionaries on this road going to Thessalonica. Apollonia was another town on this same Egnatian Road.

Thessalonica was thirty-eight miles west of Apollonia on the Egnatian Road. It was inland but it was a seaport because three rivers flowed into the sea from there. It was a prominent city of that day, another Roman colony. Cassander rebuilt it in about 315 B.C. and it is thought that he named it after Thessalonica, the stepsister of Alexander the Great. There are some warm springs there and the earlier name of the town was Therma or Therme. Cassander was one of the generals of Alexander the Great, and he took over the rule of that area after the death of Alexander. At the time of Paul, however, the city was a Roman colony.

And Paul, as his manner was, went in unto them, and three sabbath days reasoned with them out of the scriptures,

Opening and alleging, that Christ must needs have suffered, and risen again from the dead; and that this Jesus, whom I preach unto you, is Christ [Acts 17:2-3].

Paul followed his usual custom of first preaching in the synagogue. He was there only three sabbaths, which means that he could not have been there longer than a month. In that limited period of time he did his missionary work. Believers came to Christ, a local church was organized, and Paul taught them. In that brief time he taught them all the great doctrines of Scripture, including the doctrine of the Rapture of the church—we know this from his First Epistle to the Thessalonians which was the first Epistle that Paul wrote. Paul had quite a ministry there in one month's time!

Now note his message. He was "opening and alleging"—that is, from the Old Testament Scriptures—"that Christ must needs have suffered." He preached the death and resurrection of Jesus Christ, showing that this was necessary, as set forth in the Old Testament. Friend, you will not find a message given in the Book of Acts either by Peter or by Paul in which the Resurrection is not the heart of the message.

Today we find so often that the Resurrection just doesn't seem to be the heart of the message. What we talk about today is the Cross—even in fundamental circles. But, my friend, we have a living Christ today. Someone has put it this way: "There is a Man in the glory but the church has lost sight of Him." The Lord Jesus Christ is yonder at God's right hand at this very moment. That is very important. It is one thing to talk about the historical death of Christ nineteen hundred years ago and His resurrection on the third day, but the question is: How are you related to it? That was Paul's great theme in the Galatian epistle. Is it meaningful to you that Christ died and that He rose again? Are you related today to that living Christ? How has this been meshed and geared into your life?

Today we have conservatism in the church and we have liberalism in the church and, very candidly, neither group seems to be getting through to Him. Why not? Well, because every Sunday should be an Easter—on the first day of the week He came back from the dead! It is important to mention the resurrection of Christ because we are talking about the Man in the glory.

Unfortunately, that just doesn't seem to be the emphasis. Pastors don't emphasize it because seminaries don't emphasize it. Take down any theology book and study it—Strong's, Shedd's, Thornwall's, Hodge's, and you will find that all of them have a long section on the death of Christ. That's very important; thank God they have a long section on that. But they have a short section, just a few pages on the Resurrection. I think they missed the boat there. I think they should have put in a long section about the resurrection of Christ. That was the basis of New Testament preaching. I'm emphasizing this because it is very important. Paul was in Thessalonica only three Sabbath days, and the resurrection of Christ was his message.

Notice their reception of Him.

> **And some of them believed, and consorted with Paul and Silas; and of the devout Greeks a great multitude, and of the chief women not a few [Acts 17:4].**

Some of them believed. That always happens when you give out the Word of God. Some of them believe. Also some of them won't believe. The minority believe; the majority will not.

When Dr. Luke says "of the chief women not a few," he is using his usual understatement and means that a large number of prominent women came to the Lord. How wonderful!

> **But the Jews which believed not, moved with envy, took unto them certain lewd fellows of the baser sort, and gathered a company, and set all the city on an uproar, and assaulted the house of Jason, and sought to bring them out to the people [Acts 17:5].**

Unfortunately, we also have some "lewd fellows of the baser sort" in our churches today.

> **And when they found them not, they drew Jason and certain brethren unto the rulers of the city, crying, These that have turned the world upside down are come hither also [Acts 17:6].**

Now don't put that down as an oratorical gesture or hyperbole. When they said that these men were turning the world upside down, that is exactly what they meant. When Christianity penetrated that old Roman Empire it was a revolution. It had a tremendous effect.

Today we don't see much revolution except in the wrong direction. It's too bad we can't have a great revolution of turning back to the Lord

Jesus Christ and to the Word of God. Our country is a country filled
with hypocrisy. We pretend that we are a Christian nation. We pretend
that our leaders are Christian, that all the politicians are Christians,
that everyone is a Christian. Friend, we are one of the most pagan nations this world has ever known. Christianity today is mostly a pre-
tense. We need to recognize that we need to get back to the Word of
God and to the living Christ. How important that is!

**Whom Jason hath received: and these all do contrary to
the decrees of Caesar, saying that there is another king,
one Jesus.**

**And they troubled the people and the rulers of the city,
when they heard these things.**

**And when they had taken security of Jason, and of the
other, they let them go [Acts 17:7–9].**

Remember that this was a Roman colony, which was operated according to Caesar's dictates. "They had taken security of Jason" means that
he had to make bond.

PAUL'S MINISTRY AT BEREA

**And the brethren immediately sent away Paul and Silas
by night unto Berea: who coming thither went into the
synagogue of the Jews [Acts 17:10].**

You would think that all this would dampen the enthusiasm of Paul,
that it would slow him down. It didn't slow him down one bit; he is
still going. He goes to Berea, which is a town down closer to the coast.

**These were more noble than those in Thessalonica, in
that they received the word with all readiness of mind,
and searched the scriptures daily, whether those things
were so [Acts 17:11].**

These people were reasonable. They searched the Scriptures, and there came into existence a church in Berea. We don't hear much about that church. It is interesting that the strongest churches arose where the persecution was the greatest. One of the troubles today is that the church is not being persecuted. In fact, the church is just taken for granted. The average Christian is just a person to be taken for granted. It wasn't that way in the first century.

> **Therefore many of them believed; also of honourable women which were Greeks, and of men, not a few [Acts 17:12].**

Here goes Dr. Luke again with his diminutive "not a few." Why doesn't he say a great crowd of men and honorable women believed? When he says, "Not a few," he means it was a multitude.

> **But when the Jews of Thessalonica had knowledge that the word of God was preached of Paul at Berea, they came thither also, and stirred up the people.**

> **And then immediately the brethren sent away Paul to go as it were to the sea: but Silas and Timotheus abode there still [Acts 17:13–14].**

Paul continues on his way without the other members of his team.

PAUL'S MINISTRY AT ATHENS

> **And they that conducted Paul brought him unto Athens: and receiving a commandment unto Silas and Timotheus for to come to him with all speed, they departed [Acts 17:15].**

Paul goes to Athens. He will wait for Silas and Timotheus there. He probably had said to them, "You go back to check on the believers in Thessalonica and see how the church is progressing there, and check on the believers in Berea; then join me in Athens."

Now while Paul waited for them at Athens, his spirit was stirred in him, when he saw the city wholly given to idolatry [Acts 17:16].

Athens was the cultural center of the world. In fact, when one thinks of Athens, one thinks about culture. Yet it was a city filled with idolatry.

Therefore disputed he in the synagogue with the Jews, and with the devout persons, and in the market daily with them that met with him [Acts 17:17].

When I was in Athens, I went down to that market. It is right at the foot of the Acropolis. I can imagine Paul walking up and down there. He was a tentmaker, you know, and I think he sold a few tents while he was there. While he was selling the tents, he was talking about the Lord Jesus Christ. The people began to get interested.

Then certain philosophers of the Epicureans, and of the Stoics, encountered him. And some said, What will this babbler say? other some, He seemeth to be a setter forth of strange gods: because he preached unto them Jesus and the resurrection [Acts 17:18].

The philosophy of the Epicureans was more or less hedonistic. The Stoics, a group who believed in restraint, were what we today call stoical. The Epicureans believed that you go the limit, and in that way you could overcome the flesh. They thought that you should give the flesh all that it wants. If it wants liquor, drink all you can hold. Concerning sex, believe me, the Epicureans could really join in the "new morality," which was nothing new for them. By contrast, the Stoics believed that the body should be held under control.

Philosophers of both groups come to Paul to hear what he has to say. Paul has been doing a lot of talking and they call him a babbler. His subject is something new to them. Jesus and the idea of resurrection are to them "strange gods."

I hear people say today that Paul got his idea from Platonism. They say he didn't really believe in the bodily resurrection but in a platonic idea of a spiritual resurrection. It was more or less the influence of an individual permeating through society. This is the life after death. One still hears that type of thing today. It is found in liberalism, and it is nothing in the world but old Greek philosophy. But these Greeks, philosophers as they were, didn't quite understand Paul. I think Paul was a little too deep for them. Philosophy had gone to seed in Athens at this particular time. However, they wanted to hear him.

And they took him, and brought him unto Areopagus, saying, May we know what this new doctrine, whereof thou speakest, is? [Acts 17:19].

The Areopagus is a very peculiar formation of rock on top of which the Parthenon and the buildings connected with it stand. Frankly, it is a very lovely setting, beautiful buildings and beautiful statues, but a city wholly given over to idolatry. It is up from the market place of the city and Paul is brought there to speak. Probably every preacher who visits there reads Paul's sermon from the top of Mars' Hill. When I was there another preacher began to read it, and since I didn't like the way he was reading it, I went way over to the other side of the rock. I sat with my Bible and read it silently. It was a thrilling experience.

Now these Greek philosophers say to him, "May we know what this new doctrine, whereof thou speakest is?" They want to know more about it. They are completely in the dark. They are worse off than the Galatians or the people in Philippi and Thessalonica. Why? Because they think they know something. The very hardest people in the world to reach with the Word of God and the Gospel are church members because they think they don't need it. They think the Gospel is for the man on skid row and for some of their friends. Some church members can be mean and sinful and yet not recognize they really need a Savior, not only to save them from sin, but also to make their lives count for God.

For thou bringest certain strange things to our ears: we would know therefore what these things mean.

> **(For all the Athenians and strangers which were there spent their time in nothing else, but either to tell, or to hear some new thing.) [Acts 17:20-21].**

In this same way America is going to seed today. Have you ever listened to the talk shows? They are boring to tears. Everyone is trying to come up with something new. Each one is trying to say something novel. They try so hard to say something smart, something sophisticated; yet it is the same old story. Athens tried the same thing.

There must have been quite a bunch of loafers back in Athens. They didn't work—they didn't do anything. They just talked, propounding new theories and new ideas. The human family seems to reach that place of sophistication. They think they know something when they don't. They don't know the most important fact in the whole universe.

There are those who say that Paul failed on Mars' Hill, that he fell flat on his face at Athens. I totally disagree with that. I believe this was one of the greatest messages that Paul ever preached.

> **Then Paul stood in the midst of Mars' hill, and said, Ye men of Athens, I perceive that in all things ye are too superstitious [Acts 17:22].**

He begins his message quite formally, "Ye men of Athens." Then he says, "I perceive . . . ye are too superstitious." The word *superstitious* is wholly inadequate to say what Paul really means. He is saying that he perceives they are in all things too religious. The Athenians were very religious. Athens was filled with idols. There was no end to the pantheon of the Athenians and the Greeks. There were gods small and gods great; they had a god for practically everything. That is what Paul is saying. They were too religious.

I sometimes hear people ask, "Why should we send missionaries to foreign countries? Those people have their religion." I suppose that when Paul went down to Athens, somebody said, "Why are you going down there? They have religion." I am sure Paul would have answered, "That's their problem; they have too much religion." A preacher friend of mine said many years ago, "When I came to Christ, I lost my religion." There are a great many folk in our churches today who need to lose their religion so they can find Christ. That is the great problem. Some folk say, "People are too bad to be saved." The real problem is that people are too good to be saved. They think they are religious and worthy and good. My friend, we are to take the Gospel to all because all men are lost without Christ, which is the reason Paul went to Athens. The Athenians needed to hear the message of the Gospel.

Notice that in Athens Paul did not go to a synagogue. He had no springboard in Athens. He begins his masterly address to "Ye men of Athens." After he makes the observation that they are too religious, he continues:

> **For as I passed by, and beheld your devotions, I found an altar with this inscription, TO THE UNKNOWN GOD. Whom therefore ye ignorantly worship, him declare I unto you [Acts 17:23].**

"I . . . beheld your devotions." He saw their objects of worship. He noted their altars and their idols and their temples. In fact, that very beautiful temple called the Parthenon was a temple built to Athena, the virgin goddess of the Athenians. There were idols all around. Paul said, "I observed all of this, and amidst the idols I found an altar inscribed to the unknown god."

Now an altar to an unknown god could mean that the Athenians were broad-minded. They didn't want to leave anyone out. If someone had come to Athens and said, "How is it you don't have an altar to my god?" they would have answered, "Well, this altar is really to your god." That way any stranger could come to worship at the altar to the unknown god, believing it was built for his god.

Or it could mean that they recognized there was a God whom they did not know. Many pagan folk recognize that behind their idolatry is a living and true God. They know nothing about Him, and they do not know how to approach Him. They have traditions that back in the dim and distant past their ancestors did worship Him. This could have been the case with the Athenians.

Paul uses this as the springboard for his message. He says he wants to talk to them about this unknown God. He says he wants to tell them about the God whom they don't know. Perhaps that is not as diplomatic as his first approach. After all, the Athenians thought they knew everything. This crowd of philosophers met in Athens and talked back and forth, as philosophers do on college campuses today. And now Paul begins to talk to them about the God they do not know. Who is He? Well, first of all, He is the God of creation.

God that made the world and all things therein, seeing that he is Lord of heaven and earth, dwelleth not in temples made with hands [Acts 17:24].

God had made very clear all the way through the Old Testament—even when He gave to Israel the pattern for the tabernacle and the temple—that He did not dwell in one geographical spot. Solomon acknowledged this in his prayer at the dedication of the temple: "But will God indeed dwell on the earth? behold, the heaven and heaven of heavens cannot contain thee; how much less this house that I have builded?" (1 Kings 8:27). These men in the Old Testament recognized that God the Creator, the living God, could not live in a building that had been made by man. Man lives in a universe that God has made. Why does man get the idea that he can build a building for God to live in?

Neither is worshipped with men's hands, as though he needed any thing, seeing he giveth to all life, and breath, and all things [Acts 17:25].

Here is a masterly stroke by Paul. He tells them, "God doesn't need anything from you. You built an altar to Him; you bring offerings to feed Him"—they wanted this unknown God to know that they were thinking of Him. Now Paul says, "God doesn't need anything from you! God is on the giving end. He gives you life. He gives you your breath. He has given you the sun, the moon, and the stars. He has given you all things." These Athenians worshipped the sun. They said that Apollo came dragging his chariot across the sky every day. Paul says that the sun is something that God has made, and it is a gift for you. The Creator is the living God. He is the One who has given you everything. By the way, He gives you salvation also. He not only gives you physical things but also gives you spiritual gifts.

And hath made of one blood all nations of men for to dwell on all the face of the earth, and hath determined the times before appointed, and the bounds of their habitation [Acts 17:26].

So much has been made of this "one blood" business that I think we need to dissipate any wrong notions here. A better translation is, "He made from one every nation of mankind." God has made one humanity. This verse is not talking about brotherhood. The only brotherhood which Scripture knows is the brotherhood of those who are in Christ Jesus. Perhaps I should amend that by saying there is a brotherhood of sin. We all are sinners. Paul's statement that God "hath determined the times before appointed, and the bounds of their habitation" is fascinating.

Not only is He the God who created the universe and who created human beings, but it is interesting to note that he also put them in certain geographical locations.

My doctor is a cancer specialist, and he has told me to stay out of the sun here in California because I am a blonde. There seems to be even a medical reason why God put the darker races where the sun shines and put the light-skinned races up north where there is not so much sun. So some of us who are blonde and light-skinned need to be very careful about too much exposure to the sun. God is the One who has determined the geographical locations for His creatures. I guess some of my ancestors should have stayed where they belonged. Maybe I'm kind of out of place here in California, but I'm glad to be here and I try to be careful about protecting myself from too much sunshine. Now that is just a little sideline as an illustration.

God has put nations in certain places. It is interesting that the thing that has produced the wars of the past is that nations don't want to stay where they belong; they want someone else's territory. That has been the ultimate cause for every war that has ever been fought.

That they should seek the Lord, if haply they might feel after him, and find him, though he be not far from every one of us [Acts 17:27].

This phrase "feel after him" has the idea of groping after Him. Man is not really searching for the living and true God, but he is searching for a god. He is willing to put up an idol and worship it. Man is not necessarily looking for the living and true God, but he is on a search.

For in him we live, and move, and have our being; as certain also of your own poets have said, For we are also his offspring [Acts 17:28].

He does not call them sons of God but the offspring of God. He is referring to creation and the relationship to God through creation. By the way, this is not pantheism that he is stating here. He is not saying that everything is God. He says that in God we live and move and have our being, but God is beyond this created universe.

Paul quotes to them from their own poets. One of the poets he quoted was Arastus who lived about 270 B.C. He was a Stoic from Cilicia. He began a poem with an invocation to Zeus in which he said that "we too are his offspring." Cleanthes was another poet who lived about 300 B.C. He also wrote a hymn to Zeus and speaks of the fact that "we are his offspring." Paul means, of course, that we are God's creatures.

Forasmuch then as we are the offspring of God, we ought not to think that the Godhead is like unto gold, or silver, or stone, graven by art and man's device [Acts 17:29].

In other words, he says we ought not to be idolaters. He has shown God to be the Creator. Now he will present Him as the Redeemer.

And the times of this ignorance God winked at; but now commandeth all men everywhere to repent [Acts 17:30].

There was a time when God shut His eyes to paganism. Now light has come into the world. God asks men everywhere to turn to Him. Light creates responsibility. Now God is commanding all men everywhere to repent.

He has presented God as the Creator in His past work. He shows God as the Redeemer in His present work. Now he shows God as the Judge in His future work.

> **Because he hath appointed a day, in the which he will judge the world in righteousness by that man whom he hath ordained; whereof he hath given assurance unto all men, in that he hath raised him from the dead [Acts 17:31].**

When God judges, it will be right. Judgment will be through a Judge who has nail-pierced hands, the One who has been raised from the dead. Paul always presents the resurrection of Jesus Christ. The resurrection of Jesus Christ from the dead is a declaration to all men. It is by this that God assures all men there will be a judgment.

> **And when they heard of the resurrection of the dead, some mocked: and others said, We will hear thee again of this matter [Acts 17:32].**

Do you know why they mocked? Because Platonism denied the resurrection of the dead. That was one of the marks of Platonism. It denied the physical resurrection. When you hear people today talking about a *spiritual* resurrection but denying the *physical* resurrection, you are hearing Platonic philosophy rather than scriptural teaching. Paul taught the physical resurrection from the dead. So when they heard of the resurrection of the dead, some mocked.

> **So Paul departed from among them [Acts 17:33].**

Some critics have said that Paul failed at Athens. He didn't fail, friend. There will always be those who mock at the Gospel. But there will also be those who believe.

Howbeit certain men clave unto him, and believed: among the which was Dionysius the Areopagite, and a woman named Darmaris, and others with them [Acts 17:34].

There was quite an aggregation of converts in the city of Athens. When Paul went to a place and preached the Gospel, he had converts. He didn't fail. He succeeded. Wherever the Word of God is preached, there will be those who will listen and believe.

CHAPTER 18

THEME: The second missionary journey of Paul continued (Paul in Corinth; Apollos in Ephesus)

We are still on the second missionary journey of Paul. He is in Athens alone waiting for Timothy and Silas to come and join him and to bring reports from the churches in Berea and in Thessalonica. After his missionary thrust in Athens Paul goes on his journey to Corinth.

THE MINISTRY OF PAUL AT CORINTH

After these things Paul departed from Athens, and came to Corinth [Acts 18:1].

I have made the trip from Athens to Corinth by bus. Paul probably walked it. It would take a long time to walk that distance although it would be a beautiful walk. I enjoyed the scenery more since I was riding than I would have if I had been walking, I assure you. It goes past the site where the Battle of Salamis was fought at sea. This is where the Persian fleet was destroyed. There are other historical places along that way before you arrive at Corinth.

In our study of the Epistle to the Corinthians, we will see the reason Paul wrote as he did to the believers at Corinth.

For now let me say that the city of Corinth was probably the most wicked city of that day. It was the Hollywood and the Las Vegas of the Roman Empire. It was the place where you could go to live it up. Sex and drink and all other sensual pleasures were there. In Corinth today one can see the remains of a great Roman bath. That is where they went to sober up. In the distance is the temple that was dedicated to Aphrodite (or Venus) in which there were a thousand so-called vestal virgins. They were anything but virgins; they were prostitutes—sex was a religion. Corinth was one of the most wicked cities of the day. Also there were two tremendous theatres there. People came from all over the empire to the city of Corinth.

Paul came to Corinth on his second missionary journey and again on his third journey. I believe it was here where Paul had one of his most effective ministries. It is my judgment that in Corinth and Ephesus Paul had his greatest ministries. Ephesus was a religious center; Corinth was a sin center. Both cities were great commercial centers.

> **And found a certain Jew named Aquila, born in Pontus, lately come from Italy, with his wife Priscilla; (because that Claudius had commanded all Jews to depart from Rome:) and came unto them [Acts 18:2].**

In the city of Corinth he found this Jewish couple, recently come from Rome. The reason they left Rome was because of anti-Semitism which had rolled like a wave over the earth. During the days of the Roman Empire this happened several times. At this time Claudius commanded all Jews to leave Rome. Among those who got out of Rome was a very wonderful couple, Aquila and Priscilla.

> **And because he was of the same craft he abode with them, and wrought: for by their occupation they were tentmakers [Acts 18:3].**

Aquila had come there because they were in business. They opened up their shop, and one day there came to their shop a little Jew who had traveled all the way from Antioch. They got acquainted and they invited Paul to stay with them.

What do you suppose they talked about? Well, Paul led them to the Lord. In the synagogue there were others who also turned to the Lord. However, there was also great opposition against Paul among the Jews.

> **And he reasoned in the synagogue every sabbath, and persuaded the Jews and the Greeks.**

> **And when Silas and Timotheus were come from Macedonia, Paul was pressed in the spirit, and testified to the Jews that Jesus was Christ [Acts 18:4–5].**

Paul had waited in Athens for Timothy and Silas to come, but they didn't show up. Now they come to him in Corinth and bring the report from the churches in Macedonia. When we get to the first Thessalonian Epistle, we will find that Paul wrote it during this period, after he had received Timothy's report.

Now he feels that he must speak out, and he testifies that Jesus is the Messiah.

And when they opposed themselves, and blasphemed, he shook his raiment, and said unto them, Your blood be upon your own heads; I am clean: from henceforth I will go unto the Gentiles [Acts 18:6].

Apparently it was at this time that Paul made the break that took him to the Gentile world. It would seem that from this point Paul's ministry was largely to the Gentiles. We will find that true in Ephesus and less obviously in Rome.

And he departed thence, and entered into a certain man's house, named Justus, one that worshipped God, whose house joined hard to the synagogue.

And Crispus, the chief ruler of the synagogue, believed on the Lord with all his house; and many of the Corinthians hearing believed, and were baptized [Acts 18:7–8].

Paul spent about eighteen months in the city of Corinth where he had a tremendous ministry. When the Jews oppose him, He turns to the Gentiles. We find now that the Lord speaks to Paul because he is coming into a great new dimension of his missionary endeavor.

Then spake the Lord to Paul in the night by a vision, Be not afraid, but speak, and hold not thy peace:

For I am with thee, and no man shall set on thee to hurt thee: for I have much people in this city [Acts 18:9–10].

Corinth was about the last place that you would expect the Lord to "have much people." I have been through Las Vegas quite a few times. I'll be honest with you—when I look at that crowd, I wouldn't get the impression that the Lord might have people there. If the Lord were to say to me, "I have much people in this city," I wouldn't question the Lord, but it surely would be the opposite from my own impression.

Paul had already been in Corinth for quite a while, and I am sure that he was wondering about that city. I'm of the opinion that when he received this opposition, he was ready to leave and go somewhere else. However, the Lord Himself steps in and detains Paul. He tells him, "I have much people in this city."

> **And he continued there a year and six months, teaching the word of God among them [Acts 18:11].**

After Paul has had several months of ministry in Corinth, again opposition will arise.

> **And when Gallio was the deputy of Achaia, the Jews made insurrection with one accord against Paul, and brought him to the judgment seat [Acts 18:12].**

This "judgment seat" is the Bema seat. It is the Bema that Paul talks about in the Epistle to the Corinthians. I have been there and I have sat on the ruins of the Bema seat in Corinth. They brought Paul to the Bema seat, the judgment seat, and there they brought the charge against him.

> **Saying, This fellow persuadeth men to worship God contrary to the law [Acts 18:13].**

They didn't mean contrary to the law of the Roman Empire or contrary to the law of Corinth. They meant contrary to the law of the Mosaic system.

And when Paul was now about to open his mouth, Gallio said unto the Jews, If it were a matter of wrong or wicked lewdness, O ye Jews, reason would that I should bear with you:

But if it be a question of words and names, and of your law, look ye to it; for I will be no judge of such matters.

And he drave them from the judgment seat.

Then all the Greeks took Sosthenes, the chief ruler of the synagogue, and beat him before the judgment seat. And Gallio cared for none of those things [Acts 18:14–17].

I have read and heard Bible expositors condemn this man Gallio in no uncertain terms. He is pictured as an unfeeling typical judge of that day. I want to say something for the defense of Gallio. I thank God for him, and I personally think that he took the right position. I'll tell you what I mean by that. He is probably the first person who made a decision between church and state. Gallio said that if the matter was concerning religion or about some religious thing, then they should take it and handle it themselves. He was a Roman magistrate and he was concerned with enforcing Roman law. But when the case did not involve Roman law, he would not interfere. He told them to handle religious matters themselves. He adopted a "hands off" policy. I like Gallio. He separated church and state. He would not interfere with Paul preaching in the city of Corinth. Corinth was a city of freedom, including religious freedom. Since the issue had to do with religion, he asked them to settle it themselves.

Now I want to say this: I wish the Supreme Court of the United States would adopt the same policy. I wish they would adopt a "hands off" policy when it comes to matters of religion. What right does a group of secular men have to come along and make a decision that you can't have prayer in the schools? If a community wants prayer in their school, then they should have prayer in their school. If they are not having prayer in school, then the state should not force prayer in

school. We claim to have freedom of speech and freedom of religion in
our land. The unfortunate thing is that our freedoms are often curtained. They are abused and misdirected. Under the guise of separat-
ing church and state, the freedom of religion is actually curtained. If
we are going to separate church and state, then the state should keep
its nose out of that which refers to the church.

If this man Gallio were running for office, I would vote for him. I
think we need men with this kind of vision. It says Gallio cared for
none of those things. Of course not! He is a secular magistrate. He is
not going to try to settle an argument about differences in doctrine.
That's not his business, and he'll stay out of it. I would vote for him.

PAUL SAILS FOR ANTIOCH

**And Paul after this tarried there yet a good while, and
then took his leave of the brethren, and sailed thence
into Syria, and with him Priscilla and Aquila; having
shorn his head in Cenchrea: for he had a vow [Acts
18:18].**

There are a great many folk who find fault with Paul because he made
a vow. They say that this is a man who preached that we are not under
Law but we are under grace, and so he should not have made a vow.
Anyone who says this about Paul is actually making a little law for
Paul. Such folk are saying that Paul is to do things their way. Under
grace, friend, if you want to make a vow, you can make it. And if you
do not want to make a vow, you don't have to. Paul didn't force anyone
else to make a vow. In fact, he said emphatically that no one has to do
that. But if Paul wants to make a vow, that is his business. That is the
marvelous freedom that we have in the grace of God today.

There are some super-saints who form little cliques and make laws
for the Christian. They say we can't do this and we can't do that. May I
say to you very candidly that our relationship is to the Lord Jesus
Christ, and it is a love affair. If we love Him, of course we will not do
anything that will break our fellowship with Him. Don't insist that I

go through your little wicket gate; I am to follow Him. He shows me what I can and cannot do in order to maintain fellowship with Him.

If one wishes to eat meat, there is freedom to eat meat. If one wishes to observe a certain day, there is freedom to observe it. "Whether therefore ye eat, or drink, or whatsoever ye do, do all to the glory of God" (1 Cor. 10:31). The important thing is to do all to the glory of God. Eating meat will not commend you to God and neither will abstaining from meat commend you to God.

Let's not find fault with Paul here. Poor Gallio and Paul surely do get in trouble with their critics right in this particular passage. I want to defend both of them.

Paul is now returning from his second missionary journey and now he is going back to Antioch. He sails from Cenchrea, which is the seaport over on the east side. There is a canal through the Corinthian peninsula today, but there was none in that day. They would actually pull the boats overland. I have a picture taken to show the rocks that are worn by the boats which were pulled over the isthmus to the other side. Cenchrea was the port of Corinth on the eastward side. Paul goes there with Aquila and Priscilla, and they take ship there. He is not going westward any farther; he is sailing for home.

And he came to Ephesus, and left them there: but he himself entered into the synagogue, and reasoned with the Jews [Acts 18:19].

You remember that when he came out on this second journey, the Spirit of God would not allow him to come down to Ephesus. Now, on his way back, he stops at Ephesus, but he does not stay there very long.

When they desired him to tarry longer time with them, he consented not;

But bade them farewell, saying, I must by all means keep this feast that cometh in Jerusalem: but I will return again unto you, if God will. And he sailed from Ephesus [Acts 18:20–21].

Again someone may ask what business Paul has in keeping feasts. Remember his background. He is a Jew like Simon Peter. He has the background of the Mosaic system. He knows a lot of his friends will be in Jerusalem for the feast. He wants to go up to witness to them. He feels that he must by all means keep this feast that is coming in Jerusalem. He is under grace. If he wants to do that, that is his business.

However, he did see that there was a great door open in Ephesus. He has the heart of a missionary, and he wants to return to them. Ephesus was one of the great cities of the Roman Empire.

> **And when he had landed at Caesarea, and gone up, and saluted the church, he went down to Antioch [Acts 18:22].**

He landed at Caesarea. Caesarea and Joppa were the ports from which one could go up to Jerusalem. He went to Jerusalem and gave his report there. Then he went back up north to his home church, which was in Antioch. This concludes the second missionary journey of Paul.

Notice that it isn't long before he starts out on his third journey.

> **And after he had spent some time there, he departed, and went over all the country of Galatia and Phrygia in order, strengthening all the disciples [Acts 18:23].**

This is now his third trip through the Galatian country. We will find that he will go to Ephesus on his third missionary journey. He is going to have a great ministry there. But right now someone else has come into Ephesus. He is Apollos, another great preacher in the early church. He is not as well known as Paul, but we can learn a great deal about him.

APOLLOS IN EPHESUS

> **And a certain Jew named Apollos, born at Alexandria, an eloquent man, and mighty in the scriptures, came to Ephesus [Acts 18:24].**

Apollos was a Jew, which meant the had the background of the Mosaic Law. His name, *Apollos*, is Greek. So he was a Hellenist of the Diaspora. He hadn't been born in Greece or in that area of Macedonia; he was born at Alexandria in North Africa. Alexandria, founded by Alexander the Great, was one of the great centers of Greek culture. A great university was there and it had one of the finest libraries in the world. It was there that a Greek version of the Old Testament, the Septuagint, was made. There was a Jewish temple in Alexandria. The great center of the early church moved from Jerusalem and Antioch to Alexandria, and it remained important for several centuries of early church history. Athanasius, Tertullian, and Augustine, three great men of the early church, came from there. Philo, a contemporary of Apollos, mingled Greek philosophy with Judaism. This combined Platonism and Judaism. Apollos was obviously influenced by this background.

We are told that he was "an eloquent man," a great preacher. Also he was "mighty in the scriptures," which means he was well trained in the Old Testament.

> **This man was instructed in the way of the Lord; and being fervent in the spirit, he spake and taught diligently the things of the Lord, knowing only the baptism of John [Acts 18:25].**

That he had been "instructed in the way of the Lord" means he had an education by word of mouth, not by revelation. And he was "fervent in the spirit"—not the Holy Spirit. He had a passion for the things of God. This is the Holy Spirit's testimony about him. Frankly, friend, he was a great man, an outstanding man.

Apollos spoke and taught "diligently the things of the Lord." He taught everything that he had learned, but he knew only about the baptism of John. He couldn't go any further than that. He had not heard of Jesus.

> **And he began to speak boldly in the synagogue: whom when Aquila and Priscilla had heard, they took him**

**unto them, and expounded unto him the way of God
more perfectly [Acts 18:26].**

They invited Apollos home for dinner after the service. They realized
that his information was very limited; so they told him about Jesus.

**And when he was disposed to pass into Achaia, the
brethren wrote, exhorting the disciples to receive him:
who, when he was come, helped them much which had
believed through grace [Acts 18:27].**

Apollos was a brilliant man, but up until the time Aquila and Priscilla
took him home for dinner, he didn't know the Gospel of the grace of
God. Here is a case where a woman helped a preacher a great deal. She
taught him something that he didn't know.

**For he mightily convinced the Jews, and that publicly,
shewing by the scriptures that Jesus was Christ [Acts
18:28].**

PAUL'S *THIRD* MISSIONARY JOURNEY

"He mightily convinced" the Jews, showing them by the Scriptures that Jesus was Christ. He had taught zealously the things of the Old Testament up through the ministry of John the Baptist. He knew nothing beyond the baptism of John. Aquila and Priscilla had the privilege of bringing him up to date and also to conversion. He then went to Achaia, visiting the churches in Greece, including Corinth and Athens, preaching Jesus as the Messiah and Savior.

CHAPTER 19

THEME: Third missionary journey of Paul (Paul in Ephesus)

Paul's third missionary journey began in the previous chapter at verse 23 when he left Antioch. In this chapter he retraces part of his first and second missionary journeys. Then he comes to Ephesus, where he speaks daily in the school of Tyrannus for two years. Paul performs miracles which lead to the march against him led by Demetrius and his fellow silversmiths. The move is quieted by the town clerk who urges them to appeal to the law rather than resorting to violence.

PAUL'S MINISTRY IN EPHESUS

And it came to pass, that, while Apollos was at Corinth, Paul having passed through the upper coasts came to Ephesus: and finding certain disciples.

He said unto them, Have ye received the Holy Ghost since ye believed? And they said unto him, We have not so much as heard whether there be any Holy Ghost [Acts 19:1–2].

You will remember that Paul had come through Ephesus on his return trip from his second missionary journey and had told them that he would come back to them if God so willed. He had not stayed in Ephesus previously and had had no ministry there. Now he returns to Ephesus, but he has been preceded there by that great preacher, Apollos. You recall that Apollos did not know anything about the death and resurrection of Jesus Christ until Aquila and Priscilla had talked to him. All he had been preaching was the baptism of John, which was as far as his knowledge went. As a result of this, the people who had heard his preaching had been instructed only as far as the baptism of John and had not even heard of the Holy Spirit. Paul detected that.

"Have ye received the Holy Ghost *since* ye believed?" is a poor translation. Both verbs *receive* and *believe*, are in the same tense. The American Standard Version translates the verse more accurately: "Did ye receive the Holy Spirit when ye believed?" Paul is asking them, "When you believed, did you receive the Holy Spirit?" Their response was that they had not even heard that there was a Holy Spirit. They had been instructed up to the baptism of John. They had not been taught about the Lord Jesus and didn't know anything about Pentecost.

> **And he said unto them, Unto what then were ye baptized? And they said, Unto John's baptism [Acts 19:3].**

You see that these people were baptized, but they were not saved. They had not received the Holy Spirit because they were not saved. Friend, the moment you trust Christ you are regenerated by the Spirit of God, you are indwelt by the Spirit of God, you are sealed by the Spirit of God, and you are baptized into the body of believers by the Spirit of God. This happens the moment you believe and trust Christ. Paul detected that this had not happened to these people. Now Paul explains to them that they must trust the Lord Jesus to be saved. They respond to his message and many believe.

> **Then said Paul, John verily baptized with the baptism of repentance, saying unto the people, that they should believe on him which should come after him, that is, on Jesus Christ.**
>
> **When they heard this, they were baptized in the name of Jesus Christ [Acts 19:4–5].**

The baptism of John was a "baptism of repentance." It was a preparation for the coming of the Lord Jesus Christ. Now the people turn to Christ and are saved. They did not get saved under Apollos because he didn't even know about Christ when he preached to them. Some people interpret this passage to mean that they had been saved, and then later when Paul came they received the Holy Spirit. That is not true, as you can see.

> **And when Paul had laid his hands upon them, the Holy Ghost came on them; and they spake with tongues, and prophesied.**

> **And all the men were about twelve [Acts 19:6–7].**

These men could now speak the gospel in other languages—in tongues that could be understood. Ephesus was a polyglot city of the Roman Empire. There were many languages spoken there, just as there had been in Jerusalem on the Day of Pentecost. East and West met all along that coast. It was a great city of that day. These men were now able to give the good news of Christ to the entire city.

Notice there were twelve men. This was the beginning of the ministry at Ephesus. Paul had a great ministry in Corinth and an even greater ministry in Ephesus.

> **And he went into the synagogue, and spake boldly for the space of three months, disputing and persuading the things concerning the Kingdom of God.**

> **But when divers were hardened, and believed not, but spake evil of that way before the multitude, he departed from them, and separated the disciples, disputing daily in the school of one Tyrannus.**

> **And this continued by the space of two years; so that all they which dwelt in Asia heard the word of the Lord Jesus, both Jews and Greeks [Acts 19:8–10].**

Paul had to leave the synagogue because there was a great deal of opposition to him. He moved his place of operation and did his speaking daily in the school of Tyrannus.

What was this school of Tyrannus? Well, it was a school that was conducted for the Ephesians. They had a siesta in the middle of the day, probably for two or three hours. Paul, I imagine, rented the space and at siesta time, in the middle of the day, he preached the Word of God for a period of two years. As a result, the whole province of Asia heard the Word of God, both the Jews and the Greeks.

This gives us some concept of how the Word of God was growing in that day. Apparently from this vantage point the church in Colosse came into existence. You see, Paul wrote to the Colossians as he did to the Romans before he had visited them. Yet he was the founder of those churches. How could this be? By the simple fact that from the school of Tyrannus the Gospel sounded forth—it went out everywhere. When the Corinthians wanted Paul to come over to them, he wrote to them, "For I will not see you now by the way; but I trust to tarry a while with you, if the Lord permit. But I will tarry at Ephesus until Pentecost. For a great door and effectual is opened unto me, and there are many adversaries" (1 Cor. 16:7–9). For two years the Gospel sounded out so that everyone in the province of Asia had heard it. Probably the seven churches of Asia Minor came into existence through the preaching of Paul the apostle here at Ephesus. This may have been where he had his greatest ministry.

And God wrought special miracles by the hands of Paul [Acts 19:11]

There are different words used in the Greek which our Bible translates as "miracles". Here the word for "miracle" is *dunamis*, from which we get our word *dynamite*. It means "an act of power." God wrought special powers by the hands of Paul. He is exercising the gifts of an apostle.

This was a great religious center, possibly more than Athens or any other place. The great temple of Diana was there, and the worship connected with it was satanic to the very core. Now in order to meet that kind of opposition, God granted some special powers to Paul.

So that from his body were brought unto the sick handkerchiefs or aprons, and the diseases departed from them, and the evil spirits went out of them [Acts 19:12].

What were these handkerchiefs and aprons which are mentioned here? Well, actually we could call them sweat cloths. Paul used them as he worked. Remember that he was a tentmaker and this was in a warm climate. While he was working, he would be perspiring. He would use these cloths, these handkerchiefs and aprons, to wipe his brow. They were dirty. They had perspiration from his body on them. People would come and pick up these dirty cloths and would be healed of their diseases! In that area there were the mystery religions which used white garments and emphasized that everything must be very clean and white. Everything had to be just so. It seems that God was rebuking all of that sort of thing. He used these dirty sweaty cloths to heal people.

This reveals the special power that was granted to the apostle Paul. As far as I know, this is the only incident like this that ever took place—including the day in which we live. It is almost blasphemous for anyone to send out a little handkerchief and claim there is a power in it. Paul's handkerchief was an old sweat cloth. God used that to rebuke the heathen, pagan religions of that day. Diseases were healed and evil spirits went out of them when they picked up these dirty, sweaty cloths.

> **Then certain of the vagabond Jews, exorcists, took upon them to call over them which had evil spirits the name of the Lord Jesus, saying, We adjure you by Jesus whom Paul preacheth [Acts 19:13].**

When they saw what Paul did, they tried to duplicate it. Now a specific incident will be related.

> **And there were seven sons of one Sceva, a Jew, and chief of the priests, which did so.**

> **And the evil spirit answered and said, Jesus I know, and Paul I know; but who are ye? [Acts 19:14–15].**

Notice that these were priests. The priests had actually gone into this type of thing. The Greek word here for "know" is ginōskō. It does not imply a knowledge by faith. It means simply that the evil spirit knows who Jesus is.

> **And the man in whom the evil spirit was leaped on them, and overcame them, and prevailed against them, so that they fled out of that house naked and wounded [Acts 19:16].**

The attempt of the sons of Sceva to try to duplicate the miracles of Paul backfired. It backfired to their humiliation and hurt and apparently was a great embarrassment for them.

> **And this was known to all the Jews and Greeks also dwelling at Ephesus; and fear fell on them all, and the name of the Lord Jesus was magnified [Acts 19:17].**

You can see the effect that this had. It caused the name of the Lord Jesus to be spread through that entire pagan city. Ephesus was a great city, and it was shaken by this.

The miracles which Paul and the other apostles performed were not the type of thing that one hears about today. For many years there have been stories of miracles being performed in Los Angeles and in Southern California, but they made no dent or impression on this great pagan city. The miracles of Paul shook Ephesus to its very foundation. The name of the Lord Jesus was magnified through them.

> **And many that believed came, and confessed, and shewed their deeds.**

> **Many of them also which used curious arts brought their books together, and burned them before all men: and they counted the price of them, and found it fifty thousand pieces of silver [Acts 19:18–19].**

That would be about $8,000.00 U.S. currency before inflation. That is quite a bonfire, by the way, an $8,000.00 bonfire! That's what they had in Ephesus.

So mightily grew the word of God and prevailed.

After these things were ended, Paul purposed in the spirit, when he had passed through Macedonia and Achaia, to go to Jerusalem, saying, After I have been there, I must also see Rome [Acts 19:20–21].

"After these things were ended"—that is, these experiences which Dr. Luke has recorded here—it apparently was Paul's intention to go to Rome on this missionary journey. The interesting thing is that he did go to Rome, but not the way he had planned to go.

So he sent into Macedonia two of them that ministered unto him, Timotheus and Erastus; but he himself stayed in Asia for a season [Acts 19:22].

This is the time that he wrote Corinthians. Apparently Timothy and Erastus took the letter to deliver it. Although it was addressed to the Corinthians, the letter would reach the people in Macedonia, which would include Philippi and Thessalonica, and also the churches in Achaia, which would include Athens and Corinth. It was in this letter that Paul wrote that a great and effectual door was open for him in Ephesus but that there were many adversaries. We can see now that the adversaries were satanic. This was a center of pagan religion and of Satan worship. The Satan worship we see today is not something new at all.

And the same time there arose no small stir about that way [Acts 19:23].

Christianity had no name for the churches at that time—certainly no denominational name. It was simply called "that way." It was a new way, that is certain. The way was the Lord Jesus who Himself said, ". . . I am the way, the truth, and the life: no man cometh unto the Father, but by me" (John 14:6).

> **For a certain man named Demetrius, a silversmith, which made silver shrines for Diana, brought no small gain unto the craftsmen [Acts 19:24].**

The temple of Diana was a great Pagan temple, and it was the center of business. It was the bank of that day. It was also the center of sin. Gross immorality took place around it. It is true that religion can go to a lower level than anything else. That temple was one of the seven wonders of the ancient world, the largest Greek temple that was ever built. It was beautiful and it was adorned with works of art, but the image of Diana or Artemis was hideous. It was not the Diana of the Greeks, a graceful image, but was the crude, many-breasted, oriental Diana. They were selling those silver images, and it was big business. Paul's ministry was interfering with it.

> **Whom he called together with the workmen of like occupation, and said, Sirs, ye know that by this craft we have our wealth.**

> **Moreover ye see and hear, that not alone at Ephesus, but almost throughout all Asia, this Paul hath persuaded and turned away much people, saying that they be no gods, which are made with hands:**

> **So that not only this our craft is in danger to be set at nought; but also that the temple of the great goddess Diana should be despised, and her magnificence should be destroyed, whom all Asia and the world worshippeth [Acts 19:25–27].**

You can see that the uproar of the silversmiths led by Demetrius was centered, actually, around their bread and butter. They made those little images and sold them, and they were doing very well. Many people would come to the temple of Diana in Ephesus since it was one of the seven wonders of the ancient world. So these men were getting rich by selling these images. I tell you again, you cannot step on a man's pocketbook without hearing him say, "Ouch!"

The worship of Diana had spread throughout Asia. Ephesus was a center of commerce and a center of religion and a center of worship. It was a center for the Oriental and the Occidental, a place where East and West did meet—the worst in both came to Ephesus.

And when they heard these sayings, they were full of wrath, and cried out, saying, Great is Diana of the Ephesians [Acts 19:28].

They went around the city with their placards shouting, "Great is Diana of the Ephesians."

And the whole city was filled with confusion: and having caught Gaius and Aristarchus, men of Macedonia, Paul's companions in travel, they rushed with one accord into the theatre.

And when Paul would have entered in unto the people, the disciples suffered him not [Acts 19:29–30].

Paul would have been mobbed, of course. He would absolutely have been killed. He already had one experience like that over in the Galatian country when he was stoned in Lystra.

And certain of the chief of Asia, which were his friends, sent unto him, desiring him that he would not adventure himself into the theatre [Acts 19:31].

This is a mob action which is taking place. "The chief of Asia" were political or religious officials, called Asiarchs, who advised Paul against trying to address the mob. They told him it would be foolish and wouldn't do a bit of good for him to get into the mob.

Some therefore cried one thing, and some another: for the assembly was confused; and the more part knew not wherefore they were come together.

> And they drew Alexander out of the multitude, the Jews
> putting him forward. And Alexander beckoned with the
> hand, and would have made his defense unto the people
> [Acts 19:32–33].

Alexander was probably a convert who was with Paul.

> But when they knew that he was a Jew, all with one voice
> about the space of two hours cried out, Great is Diana of
> the Ephesians [Acts 19:34].

This was typical mob action. Many of them didn't even know why they
were gathered together. However, notice that they do not grant freedom
of speech to anyone else. They would not permit Alexander to speak
because they wanted to run around and squeal, "Great is Diana of the
Ephesians."

> And when the townclerk had appeased the people, he
> said, Ye men of Ephesus, what man is there that know-
> eth not how that the city of the Ephesians is a worship-
> per of the great goddess Diana, and of the image which
> fell down from Jupiter?
>
> Seeing then that these things cannot be spoken against,
> ye ought to be quiet, and to do nothing rashly [Acts
> 19:35–36].

The townclerk was, of course, a local official who told them that they
were making too much out of this whole thing. He says, "Look at this
great temple and at the great Diana. Nothing could happen to them.
Nothing could be said against them!" Now, of course, they have been
in ruins for nearly two thousand years.

> For ye have brought hither these men, which are neither
> robbers of churches, nor yet blasphemers of your god-
> dess.

> **Wherefore if Demetrius, and the craftsmen which are with him, have a matter against any man, the law is open, and there are deputies: let them implead one another [Acts 19:37–38].**

He is saying that if the silversmiths want to make a legal charge, the court is open.

> **But if ye inquire any thing concerning other matters, it shall be determined in a lawful assembly.**
>
> **For we are in danger to be called in question for this day's uproar, there being no cause whereby we may give an account of this concourse.**
>
> **And when he had thus spoken, he dismissed the assembly [Acts 19:39–41].**

He told them that if they had some issue to bring up, they should all sit down and have an orderly meeting. They were to put down their placards and quit their shouting and running around. They were actually in danger of being accused of rioting. Riots are not something new, friend. This whole scene sounds very up to date.

He dismissed the crowd. When he called their attention to what they were actually doing, the crowd broke up and the people went home. Paul's ministry in Ephesus is over now. He leaves Ephesus and goes back to Macedonia.

CHAPTER 20

THEME: Third missionary journey of Paul concluded

After Paul's experience in Ephesus, he continues on to Macedonia, to Philippi, back to Troas, and to Miletus. The elders of the church in Ephesus meet him in Miletus and they have a tender reunion and a touching farewell.

PAUL GOES INTO MACEDONIA

And after the uproar was ceased, Paul called unto him the disciples, and embraced them, and departed for to go into Macedonia.

And when he had gone over those parts, and had given them much exhortation, he came into Greece [Acts 20:1–2].

This means that he revisited Athens and Corinth.

And there abode three months. And when the Jews laid wait for him, as he was about to sail into Syria, he purposed to return through Macedonia.

And there accompanied him into Asia Sopater of Berea; and of the Thessalonians, Aristarchus and Secundus; and Gaius of Derbe, and Timotheus; and of Asia, Tychicus and Trophimus [Acts 20:3–4].

The men named are all believers who had come to Christ under the ministry of Paul. He has quite a delegation now. These men have become missionaries.

We need to recognize that when Paul went through Greece and Macedonia, he visited all the churches which he had founded there.

He would have stopped at Athens and Corinth, at Thessalonica and Berea and Philippi. So he retraced his steps and visited all the churches that were in Europe—or at least in the European section of his third journey.

PAUL AT TROAS

You may remember that Troas was the springboard from which Paul leaped into Europe on his second missionary journey. Now he comes back to Troas on his last missionary journey.

These going before tarried for us at Troas [Acts 20:5].

The "us" indicates that Dr. Luke stays with Paul while the others go ahead of them to Troas.

This is quite a group of men, missionaries, who worked with Paul. I take it that these men had been traveling with Paul before. When Paul would have a ministry in a place like Corinth, probably these men would radiate out and have a ministry in the countryside and the small towns. We read in the Epistle to the Colossians about the fact that the Word of God had sounded out in that day to the whole world. That sounds unbelievable, but it was true. It was no oratorical gesture. Of course "the whole world" means the Roman world because that was the world of that day. The Word of God had spread throughout the Roman world. We get some insight here and recognize that there were other people working with the apostles. Acts traces the work of Peter and Paul as the dominant ones—Peter as the Apostle to the Jews and Paul as the Apostle to the Gentiles. What we have here in the Book of Acts is a very limited account of the missionary work that was going on.

And we sailed away from Philippi after the days of unleavened bread, and came unto them to Troas in five days; where we abode seven days [Acts 20:6].

It is interesting that the trip that took them five days to make can now be made by tourists in about fifty minutes. How different transportation is today! Transportation is more efficient, but our ministry is certainly not as effective.

And upon the first day of the week, when the disciples came together to break bread, Paul preached unto them, ready to depart on the morrow; and continued his speech until midnight [Acts 20:7].

There are several things I want to say about this verse. I want you to note that it was upon the first day of the week that they came together. Where we have a record of the day on which the early church met, it was always the first day of the week. Paul tells the Corinthians that they are to bring their gifts on the first day of the week (see 1 Cor. 16:2). In our verse in Acts here it says that "when the disciples came together to break bread" it was "upon the *first* day of the week." This means that they celebrated the Lord's Supper on Sunday. It was on this day that Paul preached to them. The early church met on the first day of the week. That was the important day because it was the day when Jesus came back from the dead. Under the old creation the seventh day was the important day, the Sabbath day. That belongs to the old creation. On the Sabbath day Jesus was dead, inside the tomb. On the first day of the week He came forth. We meet on that day because we are now joined to a living Christ. That is the testimony of the first day of the week.

Now the other thing that interests me about this verse is that Paul was going to leave them the next day; so he preached all the way to midnight. Now, I do not know any congregation that would listen to me until midnight. I'm of the opinion that there aren't many preachers who would preach until midnight in these days in which we live. However, this is Paul's last visit. It is a tender meeting. He is getting ready to leave and he will not be back. This gives him an excuse to preach that long.

I tell congregations very frankly that I'm a long-winded preacher. I'm known as that. I love to teach the Word of God. I have a system of homiletics that I never learned in the seminary. I picked it up myself— in fact, I got it from a cigarette commercial. This is it: It's not how long you make it but how you make it long. I believe in making it long; my scriptural authority for it is that Paul did it. He spoke until midnight. You can't help but smile at that.

> **And there were many lights in the upper chamber, where they were gathered together [Acts 20:8].**

They had the place all lighted up. These early Christians didn't stay up until midnight whooping it up, but they were still up at midnight listening to the Word of God and praising Him. May I say to you that we have let the world take away from us the fun that we ought to be having today with the things of God. So if your preacher goes a little overtime, friend, be patient with him. However, I think midnight was a little long for the apostle Paul to preach, because look what happened here.

> **And there sat in a window a certain young man named Eutychus, being fallen into a deep sleep: and as Paul was long preaching, he sunk down with sleep, and fell down from the third loft, and was taken up dead [Acts 20:9].**

A friend of mine who preached up in the country of middle Tennessee invited me to come there to hold some meetings in his church. In the summertime they would have quite protracted meetings at their Bible conference. It was interesting that in the back of the church there was a place for several pallets. When a little fellow would go to sleep, the mother holding him would simply get up and take him to the back of the room and put him down on the pallet. When another little fellow would go to sleep, his mother would get up with him and do the same thing. There would be six or more children asleep in the back of that church. One night after several mothers had put their children down on the pallet, my friend interrupted his message and remarked, "I'm a better preacher than the apostle Paul! Paul preached until midnight and he put only one to sleep. I'm preaching here until about nine o'clock and I've already put four to sleep!"

I confess that Paul's experience has always been a comfort to me. When I look out at the congregation and see some brother or sister out there sound asleep, I say to myself, "It's all right. Just let them sleep. Paul put them to sleep, too."

Can't you just see this Eutychus? It says that "he sunk down with sleep." He was sound asleep, and I can imagine that he was snoring. He fell from the third loft—which means he was higher than the second floor. It is no longer a laughable experience. If this had been the end, it would have been a tragedy. But notice what happens.

> **And Paul went down, and fell on him, and embracing him said, Trouble not yourselves; for his life is in him.**
>
> **When he therefore was come up again, and had broken bread, and eaten, and talked a long while, even till break of day, so he departed.**
>
> **And they brought the young man alive, and were not a little comforted [Acts 20:10–12].**

Paul raised this boy from the dead. You will remember also that Simon Peter raised Dorcas from the dead. This was a gift that belonged to the apostles. After the canon of Scripture was established, the sign gifts were not manifested—they disappeared from the church. When Dr. Luke writes that they "were not a little comforted," he means they were really thrilled that this precious young man had been raised from the dead and was back in their midst. And now Paul continues to preach through the night even until daybreak. What a rebuke that is to us! In some churches there is a chorus of complaint if a pastor preaches ten or even five minutes longer than usual. These early believers sat up all night listening to Paul. I know someone is going to say, "If I could listen to Paul, I'd listen all night, too." Probably Paul was nothing more than a humble preacher of the Gospel. We do know that Apollos was an eloquent man, but that is not said of Paul. These believers simply wanted to hear the Word of God. How wonderful that is!

PAUL AT MILETUS

And we went before to ship, and sailed unto Assos, there intending to take in Paul: for so had he appointed, minding himself to go afoot [Acts 20:13].

Now they are traveling again. Dr. Luke and others of the group sailed to Assos but Paul traveled on foot. Why do you suppose Paul did that? Well, I'm sure it was so that he could witness along the way. I think as he walked, there were many places along the way where he would stop to witness to people.

And when he met with us at Assos, we took him in, and came to Mitylene.

And we sailed thence, and came the next day over against Chios; and the next day we arrived at Samos, and tarried at Trogyllium; and the next day we came to Miletus [Acts 20:14–15].

Now there is a good exercise in pronunciation as well as a little study in geography. I hope you will follow these journeys of Paul on a map. They make a nice little travelog.

For Paul had determined to sail by Ephesus, because he would not spend the time in Asia: for he hasted, if it were possible for him, to be at Jerusalem the day of Pentecost [Acts 20:16].

Paul wants to be in Jerusalem for the feast of Pentecost; so he is in a hurry. However, he was determined not to miss Ephesus. He stops at Miletus, which is the port of Ephesus.

And from Miletus he sent to Ephesus, and called the elders of the church [Acts 20:17].

A good map will show you that Ephesus was actually a little inland. The river there slowly filled up the harbor at Ephesus. Today the city of Ephesus is actually inland about two or three miles from the water's edge. A great part of the city is as much as five miles inland. Miletus is right down on the coast. Paul sent for the elders of Ephesus to come to Miletus to meet him there.

And when they were come to him, he said unto them, Ye know, from the first day that I came into Asia, after what manner I have been with you at all seasons,

Serving the Lord with all humility of mind, and with many tears, and temptations, which befell me by the lying in wait of the Jews:

And how I kept back nothing that was profitable unto you, but have shewed you, and have taught you publicly, and from house to house.

Testifying both to the Jews, and also to the Greeks, repentance toward God, and faith toward our Lord Jesus Christ [Acts 20:18–21].

Paul was a faithful witness for Jesus Christ. He pulled no punches. He could declare that he had given them the Word of God, the total Word of God. I am not the first one to have a through the Bible program—Paul taught it all. He gave to them the full counsel of God. He was faithful even in the face of opposition by the religious rulers of the Jews.

And now, behold, I go bound in the spirit unto Jerusalem, not knowing the things that shall befall me there:

Save that the Holy Ghost witnesseth in every city, saying that bonds and afflictions abide me.

> **But none of these things move me, neither count I my life
> dear unto myself, so that I might finish my course with
> joy, and the ministry, which I have received of the Lord
> Jesus, to testify the gospel of the grace of God [Acts
> 20:22–24].**

Here is a point over which many great teachers of the Bible differ.
Some of my good friends in the ministry and many good, authoritative
Bible teachers believe that Paul made a mistake in going to Jerusalem.
They think that he should not have gone. However, this testimony
which Paul gives is very clear. I believe that he was entirely in the will
of God in going to Jerusalem. He is saying in effect, "I am going to
Jerusalem. I am bound in the spirit because everywhere I have gone,
the Spirit of God has shown me that bonds and affliction await me in
Jerusalem." Now that is different from Acts 16 when he was forbidden
by the Spirit of God to preach in Asia. In fact, God simply put up
roadblocks which directed him to Europe. There is no roadblock here.
Rather, the Spirit of God is revealing to Paul what he will be walking
into when he reaches Jerusalem. Paul makes it clear that he realizes he
will suffer if he goes to Jerusalem. He says, "I don't count my life dear.
I'm willing to lay down my life for Jesus." He wanted to bring the gift
to the poor saints in Jerusalem in his own hands. In his swan song Paul
wrote, "I have finished my course." I think Paul touched all the bases.
Jerusalem was one of those bases.

> **And now, behold, I know that ye all, among whom I
> have gone preaching the kingdom of God, shall see my
> face no more.**
>
> **Wherefore I take you to record this day, that I am pure
> from the blood of all men.**
>
> **For I have not shunned to declare unto you all the coun-
> sel of God [Acts 20:25–27].**

Paul knew that he would not see these folk again in this life. Paul also
knew that he had honestly given to them the entire counsel of God.

As I write this, I am a retired preacher. I have made many blunders and have failed in many ways. But as I look back on my ministry, I can say truthfully that when I stood in the pulpit, I declared the Word of God as I saw it. I have the deep satisfaction of knowing that if I went back to any pulpit which I have held, I haven't a thing to add to what I have already said. I don't mean I couldn't say it in a better way, but the important thing is that I declared the whole counsel of God. I have always believed that the important issue is to get out the entire Word of God.

Take heed therefore unto yourselves, and to all the flock, over the which the Holy Ghost hath made you overseers, to feed the church of God, which he hath purchased with his own blood [Acts 20:28].

This is the business of the officers of the church. They are not to run the church, but they are to see that the church is fed the Word of God.

For I know this, that after my departing shall grievous wolves enter in among you, not sparing the flock.

Also of your own selves shall men arise, speaking perverse things, to draw away disciples after them [Acts 20:29–30].

Friend, I have seen that happen. The Devil wants to get into a church where the Bible has been taught. He would like to wreck a radio ministry that is teaching the Word of God. The Devil is not our friend; he is our enemy. He wants to stop the teaching of God's Word. Paul warned them at Ephesus that this would happen to them. He tells them there will be little termites right in their midst who will really cause trouble for them.

Therefore watch, and remember, that by the space of three years I ceased not to warn every one night and day with tears.

> **And now brethren, I commend you to God, and to the word of his grace, which is able to build you up, and to give you an inheritance among all them which are sanctified [Acts 20:31-32].**

He commends them to God and to the Word of His grace. That is what we can do whenever we leave our people.

> **I have coveted no man's silver, or gold, or apparel.**
>
> **Yea, ye yourselves know, that these hands have ministered unto my necessities, and to them that were with me [Acts 20:33-34].**

Paul was not covetous of money. He worked in order to support himself and those who were with him.

> **I have shewed you all things, how that so labouring ye ought to support the weak, and to remember the words of the Lord Jesus, how he said, It is more blessed to give than to receive.**
>
> **And when he had thus spoken, he kneeled down, and prayed with them all.**
>
> **And they all wept sore, and fell on Paul's neck, and kissed him.**
>
> **Sorrowing most of all for the words which he spake, that they should see his face no more. And they accompanied him unto the ship [Acts 20:35-38].**

This is a tender meeting between Paul and the elders of the church in Ephesus. These men love Paul and he loves them. It is difficult for them to let him go, knowing that they will not see him again in this life. They bid him a touching farewell.

CHAPTER 21

THEME: Paul goes to Jerusalem and is arrested

Paul has made three missionary journeys. He is returning now, and it is almost like a wonderful victory march as he comes back into the city of Jerusalem. But along the way warnings are coming to him. He knows that trouble awaits him in Jerusalem.

Chapter 20 concluded with the tender meeting he had with the Ephesian elders at Miletus. Now he boards ship for the voyage that will return him to Israel.

PAUL AT TYRE

And it came to pass, that after we were gotten from them, and had launched, we came with a straight course unto Coos, and the day following unto Rhodes, and from thence unto Patara:

And finding a ship sailing over unto Phenicia, we went aboard, and set forth [Acts 21:1–2].

Are you following him? He took a ship at Miletus and they sailed down to the southern coast of Asia Minor to Patara. There they changed ships. Now he is headed for Tyre on the seacoast north of Caesarea. It was actually on the coast of Israel in what was ancient Phoenicia. Today that is Lebanon.

Now when we had discovered Cyprus, we left it on the left hand, and sailed into Syria, and landed at Tyre: for there the ship was to unlade her burden [Acts 21:3].

I love the way this is expressed here. I think the translators of our Authorized Version have captured something that the modern translations just miss. They "discovered Cyprus" on the left hand is a way of saying that as they were sailing towards Tyre, Cyprus loomed up in the distance on their left-hand side. Of course it doesn't mean that they were the first people to discover Cyprus. They saw the island and were near enough to recognize it, but they did not stop there. They were on their way to Tyre, a great commercial center which had been there since ancient times.

> **And finding disciples, we tarried there seven days: who said to Paul through the Spirit, that he should not go up to Jerusalem [Acts 21:4].**

This is the verse used by those Bible teachers who feel that Paul made a great mistake when he went up to Jerusalem. It shows that these men spoke to Paul through the Holy Spirit. If I understand this correctly, the Spirit of God is not going to contradict Himself. I believe He is saying the same thing here that He had said before. Paul is not to go up to Jerusalem unless he is prepared to make the required sacrifice. Paul keeps saying that he is willing to make the sacrifice. He is perfectly willing to lay down his life for the Lord Jesus. That is the way I think it should be understood.

For several reasons, I do not believe that Paul stepped out of the will of God when he went up to Jerusalem. He had a sentimental reason for going there, but it was a good reason. He was carrying the offering from the gentile Christians to the suffering saints in Jerusalem. He wanted to present this to the church in Jerusalem with his own hands, because it was his hands that at one time had wasted the church in Jerusalem. He had been partly responsible for the state of penury in which the saints in Jerusalem found themselves. Paul did not want to send some representative to Jerusalem; he wanted to go to Jerusalem himself.

Another reason I do not believe that Paul stepped out of the will of God is because of his writings later on. When Paul was in prison in Rome, the church at Philippi sent to him an expression of their sympathy. They loved him and they sympathized with his condition. But Paul wrote to them, "But I would ye should understand, brethren, that the things which happened unto me have fallen out rather unto the furtherance of the gospel" (Phil. 1:12). Because what happened to Paul did not hinder the spread of the gospel, I do not believe that Paul was out of the will of God.

Furthermore, you remember that when the Lord appeared to Ananias and told him to go to Paul after his conversion, He said to Ananias, ". . . Go thy way: for he is a chosen vessel unto me, to bear my name before the Gentiles, and kings, and the children of Israel: For I will shew him how great things he must suffer for my name's sake" (Acts 9:15–16). Up to this point in our study of Acts, Paul has not appeared before kings and rulers, but we know it is in the will of God that he should do so. In the next chapters we will find that he does go before kings. He will testify before King Agrippa. It is probable that he appeared before Nero in Rome. We know for certain that he reached those who were in Caesar's household because he sent greetings from them in his Epistle to the Philippians (4:22), which was written while he was a prisoner in Rome.

Finally, as I have already mentioned, in 2 Timothy 4:7 Paul writes, ". . . I have finished my course. . . ." This was written at the end of his life. It seems to me that he would not say that if for a time he had stepped out of the will of God. I must confess that as I look back over my own ministry, I am confident that I stepped out of the will of God for a brief time. I didn't do it purposely. I did it ignorantly. I did it in a headstrong manner. I think the Lord has a way of making these things up to us. But I do not think that Paul at the end of his life could write that he had finished his course if he had been out of the will of God.

I have spent some time on this because there is controversy over it. I have several very good friends in the ministry who do not agree with my point of view, but we are still friends. I love these brethren in the Lord. I just tease them and say I hope they will see the light someday. As one of them said to me, "When we get in the presence of the Lord, we will all be in agreement."

And when we had accomplished those days, we departed and went our way; and they all brought us on our way, with wives and children, till we were out of the

**city: and we kneeled down on the shore, and prayed
[Acts 21:5].**

Again, this is a lovely thing that Paul did here. Paul and the people
with him kneeled down there on the shore and prayed.

Friend, the best position to be in while praying is kneeling. However, you can pray in any posture and anywhere. Since I drive a great
deal, I have learned to pray in the car. (When you drive the freeways of
Southern California, you had better learn to pray!) But the most appropriate posture when we come into the presence of Almighty God is to
kneel.

**And when we had taken our leave one of another, we
took ship; and they returned home again.**

**And when we had finished our course from Tyre, we
came to Ptolemais, and saluted the brethren, and abode
with them one day [Acts 21:6-7].**

I have often wondered why Paul didn't stay there longer than that. You
will notice the marvelous reception given to him and the number of
believers in all these various places at that time. There must have been
millions of believers in the Roman Empire by the end of the first century.

PAUL AT CAESAREA

**And the next day we that were of Paul's company de-
parted, and came unto Caesarea: and we entered into
the house of Philip the evangelist, which was one of the
seven; and abode with him [Acts 21:8].**

Paul is traveling down the coastline going from one place to another. I
have driven that route by bus. Since there was no bus running in Paul's
day, I'm sure that he walked this route. And what a ministry he had!
Think of the believers that he met on the way. He had a real ministry
and a real opportunity.

As I have been going from church to church, from town to town, from city to city, from place to place, ministering the Word of God, it is a great encouragement to see what God is doing in the lives of folk. When I was a pastor, I had to keep my nose to the grindstone, and I developed an Elijah complex—"I'm the only one left. I'm all by myself. I am the only one standing for you, Lord." Friend, if you could go over the ground I have been over in the past year, it would thrill your heart to know the number of wonderful churches, wonderful Christian works, wonderful Christian homes, wonderful Christian believers that there are in this country and in other countries of the world. It has been a real thrill to my own heart to meet these believers. Undoubtedly this was also the experience of Paul.

And the same man had four daughters, virgins, which did prophesy [Acts 21:9].

Philip was an *evangelist*. The word literally means "one who announces good tidings." This verse shows that women did occupy a prominent place in the church. These particular women had the gift of prophecy. The New Testament had not been written as yet; so the gift of prophecy was needed in the early church.

And as we tarried there many days, there came down from Judaea a certain prophet, named Agabus.

And when he was come unto us, he took Paul's girdle, and bound his own hands and feet, and said, Thus saith the Holy Ghost, So shall the Jews at Jerusalem bind the man that owneth this girdle, and shall deliver him into the hands of the Gentiles [Acts 21:10–11].

The Holy Spirit is revealing to Paul what will happen to him when he goes up to Jerusalem. It is as though He is saying, "Paul, this is what you are going to face. Are you willing to do it?" God doesn't want Paul to feel that He let him stumble unwittingly into a trap. Paul knows what awaits him, and he still is perfectly willing to go. Actually, this prophet is not telling him anything new. Back in chapter 20, when he was still in Asia Minor, he already knew that bonds and afflictions waited for him.

> **And when we heard these things, both we, and they of that place, besought him not to go up to Jerusalem.**

> **Then Paul answered, what mean ye to weep and to break mine heart? for I am ready not to be bound only, but also to die at Jerusalem for the name of the Lord Jesus [Acts 21:12–13].**

Remember that this is Dr. Luke writing. He and the others didn't want to see Paul go to Jerusalem. The Spirit of God is revealing to Paul that he is going to be bound. Paul is not only willing to be bound but is also willing to die for Jesus in Jerusalem. He asks the believers not to cry and to break his heart. It is touching here to see the concern of the believers for the apostle Paul. My, how they loved him!

> **And when he would not be persuaded, we ceased, saying, The will of the Lord be done [Acts 21:14].**

And I think the will of the Lord was done.

PAUL AT JERUSALEM

> **And after those days we took up our carriages, and went up to Jerusalem.**

> **There went with us also certain of the disciples of Caesarea, and brought with them one Mnason of Cyprus, an old disciple, with whom we should lodge.**

> **And when we were come to Jerusalem, the brethren received us gladly [Acts 21:15–17].**

Notice that when the apostle Paul came to Jerusalem, the church that was there received him gladly.

And the day following Paul went in with us unto James; and all the elders were present [Acts 21:18].

What a glorious reception by the church in Jerusalem! He is a veteran now, friend. He has been in the ministry of the Lord Jesus Christ, and he bears in his body the marks of the Lord Jesus.

And when he had saluted them, he declared particularly what things God had wrought among the Gentiles by his ministry.

And when they heard it, they glorified the Lord, and said unto him, Thou seest, brother, how many thousands of Jews there are which believe; and they are all zealous of the law:

And they are informed of thee, that thou teachest all the Jews which are among the Gentiles to forsake Moses, saying that they ought not to circumcise their children, neither to walk after the customs [Acts 21:19–21].

The Jews twisted a little what Paul was actually doing. Paul did not really teach the things that they claimed he was teaching.

We come now to another interesting passage about which good Bible expositors offer different explanations. Was Paul out or in the will of God when he went to Jerusalem and took a Jewish vow that evidently involved a sacrifice?

The believers here in Jerusalem speak of the thousands of Jewish converts to Christ. These Jews who had found their completion in Jesus Christ had not forsaken the Mosaic Law. However, they could not insist that Gentiles must come under the Law. On the other hand, Gentiles could not insist that the Jews forsake the *practices* of the Law— *provided they were not trusting them for salvation.* Those who insist that the grace of God did not force the Gentiles to keep the Mosaic Law seem to forget that the same grace permits the Jew to continue in its precepts if he feels it is the will of God.

For example, we know that Peter had eaten nothing contrary to Mo-

saic Law until he visited Paul in Antioch. Also, Jewish believers had
an abhorrence of eating anything that had been sacrificed to idols.
This did not bother the conscience of the Gentile. However, if the eating of such meat offended the conscience of another believer and
caused him to stumble, then it was wrong. Paul makes it very clear that
meat does not commend us to God. "But meat commendeth us not to
God: for neither, if we eat, are we the better; neither, if we eat not, are
we the worse" (1 Cor. 8:8).

Paul also wrote that if a person was brought up under certain customs, the grace of God allows him to follow those customs after he has
accepted the Lord Jesus as his Savior. "But as God hath distributed to
every man, as the Lord hath called every one, so let him walk. And so
ordain I in all churches. Is any man called being circumcised? let him
not become uncircumcised. Is any called in uncircumcision? let him
not be circumcised. Circumcision is nothing, and uncircumcision is
nothing, but the keeping of the commandments of God. Let every man
abide in the same calling wherein he was called" (1 Cor. 7:17–20).

Paul applies this principle in winning people for Christ. "For
though I be free from all men, yet have I made myself servant unto all,
that I might gain the more. And unto the Jews I became as a Jew, that I
might gain the Jews; to them that are under the law, as under the law,
that I might gain them that are under the law; To them that are without
law, as without law, (being not without law to God, but under the law
to Christ,) that I might gain them that are without law. To the weak
became I as weak, that I might gain the weak: I am made all things to
all men, that I might by all means save some. And this I do for the
gospel's sake, that I might be partaker thereof with you" (1 Cor.
9:19–23). I do not think that we should criticize Paul for what he does
here in Jerusalem. Grace permitted Paul to take a Jewish vow to win the
Jews. If he had been a Gentile, it would have been questionable for him
to adopt a foreign custom.

With that as a background, we understand Paul's action.

**What is it therefore? the multitude must needs come to-
gether: for they will hear that thou art come.**

Do therefore this that we say to thee: We have four men which have a vow on them;

Them take, and purify thyself with them, and be at charges with them, that they may shave their heads: and all may know that those things, whereof they were informed concerning thee, are nothing; but that thou thyself also walkest orderly, and keepest the law.

As touching the Gentiles which believe, we have written and concluded that they observe no such thing, save only that they keep themselves from things offered to idols, and from blood, and from strangled, and from fornication.

Then Paul took the men, and the next day purifying himself with them entered into the temple, to signify the accomplishment of the days of purification, until that an offering should be offered for every one of them [Acts 21:22–26].

Now what should Paul do? He has arrived at Jerusalem and has been given a royal reception by the church. He has given them the gift from the gentile churches. They have listened to his report and rejoiced in the way God has saved the Gentiles. Now they turn to Paul and tell him that there are thousands of Jews in Jerusalem who are trusting Christ and have accepted Him as their Messiah and Savior. None of them want to have a division in the church. There is only one church of Jesus Christ, not a Jewish church and a gentile church. A Jew who comes to Jesus Christ does not stop being a Jew. So they say to Paul, "Look, you are a Jew. That is your background. And you want to win the Jews for Christ." Paul says, "I sure do!" So they say, "Since you are a Jew, it wouldn't hurt you to go with these four Jewish men who have made a vow. They have shaved their heads and are going into the temple. Would you go along with them?" Paul says, "Sure."

Paul didn't take this vow because he was commanded to do so. He took this vow because he wanted to win these people.

Friend, you don't have to take a vow. But if you want to take a vow, you can. If you want to shave your head with a vow, that is your business. If you want to take a vow and let your hair grow long, that is your business. It is all right with the Lord. Under grace you have a right to do these things. Under grace you have the right to make a vow if you want to do so—just so you understand that you are not *saved* by what you do, but by the grace of God.

PAUL IN THE TEMPLE AT JERUSALEM

And when the seven days were almost ended, the Jews which were of Asia, when they saw him in the temple, stirred up all the people, and laid hands on him.

Crying out, Men of Israel, help: This is the man, that teacheth all men every where against the people, and the law, and this place: and further brought Greeks also into the temple, and hath polluted this holy place [Acts 21:27–28]

As mobs generally do, this mob acts on assumption and misinformation.

(For they had seen before with him in the City Trophimus an Ephesian, whom they supposed that Paul had brought into the temple.) [Acts 21:29].

Here we find this distinction that we need to make. Paul, a Jew, brought up in that tradition, went to the temple when he came to Jerusalem. Trophimus who was a gentile Ephesian, apparently a convert through the ministry of Paul, when he was in Jerusalem with Paul, would have no inclination to go to the temple or take part in any ritual in the temple. That was not part of his background. Under grace he could have if he had wanted to. This is what I mean by our freedom under grace. Of course Paul knew that the vow he was taking had no bearing on his salvation. Both Jew and Gentile are saved only and alone by the grace of God through Jesus Christ.

Paul's vow probably included fasting and eating certain foods. That was a part of his background. Today as I travel around, I find that a great many Christians are diet faddists. It always amazes me to find how many there are. They are constantly telling me their advice about what this or that diet will do for me. May I say that the only difference a diet will make is in your physical body. A diet will not commend you to God. Under grace you can go on a diet or not go on a diet. It may have something to do with your health and your physical condition. It has nothing to do with your relationship to God. O, if God's people could only learn that!

> And all the city was moved, and the people ran together: and they took Paul, and drew him out of the temple: and forthwith the doors were shut.

> And as they went about to kill him, tidings came unto the chief captain of the band, that all Jerusalem was in an uproar.

> Who immediately took soldiers and centurions, and ran down unto them: and when they saw the chief captain and the soldiers, they left beating of Paul [Acts 21:30–32].

Notice their bitterness and hatred of Paul. They hate him because he is teaching that one does not need to go through the Mosaic system to be saved. Paul is right in following one of the customs of his people if he wants to. He is trying to win his own people. Although it didn't accomplish the purpose that he had in mind, I think it accomplished a God-given purpose.

The mob would have killed Paul if the captain and the soldiers had not intervened.

PAUL BOUND IN CHAINS

> Then the chief captain came near, and took him, and commanded him to be bound with two chains; and de-

manded who he was, and what he had done [Acts 21:33].

This captain did not know Paul at all. He didn't cry out, "Oh, this is Paul, the great Apostle to the Gentiles." He wasn't looking upon him like that at all. He didn't know who he was and actually thought that he had committed some crime; so he put him in chains.

> **And some cried one thing, some another, among the multitude: and when he could not know the certainty for the tumult, he commanded him to be carried into the castle.**
>
> **And when he came upon the stairs, so it was, that he was borne of the soldiers for the violence of the people.**
>
> **For the multitude of the people followed after, crying, Away with him [Acts 21:34–36].**

Since the captain couldn't learn anything from the mob, he took Paul to the castle in order to find out what the charge was against him. The mob was not willing to settle for anything less than the death of Paul.

> **And as Paul was to be led into the castle, he said unto the chief captain, May I speak unto thee? Who said, canst thou speak Greek? [Acts 21:37].**

The captain was amazed. He thought that he had bound a common criminal, but this man speaks a fluent Greek. The captain understood that because he was a foreign emissary.

> **Art not thou that Egyptian, which before these days madest an uproar, and leddest out into the wilderness four thousand men that were murderers? [Acts 21:38].**

He thought that Paul was a mob leader, one of the protesters taking a mob out into the country.

> But Paul said, I am a man which am a Jew of Tarsus, a
> city in Cilicia, a citizen of no mean city: and, I beseech
> thee, suffer me to speak unto the people [Acts 21:39].

Paul speaks Greek, but he informs the captain that he is a Jew. When
the captain learns who Paul is, he says, "Well, sure. I didn't know who
you were. Go ahead and speak to them."

> And when he had given him license, Paul stood on the
> stairs, and beckoned with the hand unto the people.
> And when there was made a great silence, he spake unto
> them in the Hebrew tongue, saying [Acts 21:40].

Although Paul speaks to the captain in Greek, when he addresses this
Jewish mob, he speaks in their native tongue, Hebrew. And the minute
he begins to address them in Hebrew, the language they love and understand, they listen to him.

CHAPTER 22

THEME: Paul's defense before the mob at Jerusalem

This chapter gives Paul's message before the mob. He recounts his encounter with Christ and his subsequent experience which brought him to Jerusalem. Then Paul appeals to his Roman citizenship to deliver himself from the awful whipping of a prisoner.

Let us listen to Paul. Here is a great message of the apostle Paul.

PAUL'S DEFENSE BEFORE THE MOB

Men, brethren, and fathers, hear ye my defense which I make now unto you [Acts 22:1].

"Men?" Yes. "Brethren?" Yes, they belong to the same race. Yet these brethren want to kill him. Is he being sarcastic? No, because then he shows respect for the elder men, "and fathers."

(And when they heard that he spake in the Hebrew tongue to them, they kept the more silence: and he saith) [Acts 22:2].

The minute he begins to speak in Hebrew, they become quiet. It is like a raging wind suddenly dying down, like calming the waves of the seas. They are listening to a man who is one of them. He begins with his personal history.

I am verily a man which am a Jew, born in Tarsus, a city in Cilicia, yet brought up in this city at the feet of Gamaliel, and taught according to the perfect manner of the law of the fathers, and was zealous toward God, as ye all are this day [Acts 22:3].

Paul is being persecuted by the Jewish leaders, by the religious leaders of that day. Paul shows them that he had been one of them—he had been a Pharisee. One of the reasons he has so much sympathy for them and is so loving toward them is that he knows exactly how they feel. He is giving them his background because he wants to win them for Christ.

Paul had a tremendous background. Tarsus was actually the center of Greek learning of that day. The finest Greek university in Paul's day was in Tarsus, not in Athens or Corinth, which had passed their zeniths. Tarsus was a thriving Greek city and an educational center.

Undoubtedly Paul had been brought up in that university in Tarsus and had a Greek background, but he had also been in Jerusalem where he had studied under Gamaliel. They are listening to him now.

> **And I persecuted this way unto the death, binding and delivering into prisons both men and women [Acts 22:4].**

Notice that Paul calls it "this way" again. He doesn't mention the church or the followers of Christ or Christians. He uses the term which they understand and which he understands. I think "this way" is still a good term to use. What is "this way?" Well, it is the Way, the Truth, and the Life. It is the person of the Lord Jesus.

He is saying to them, "Listen, I have the same background you folk have. I persecuted this way. I know how you feel. I did the same thing."

> **As also the high priest doth bear me witness, and all the estate of the elders: from whom also I received letters unto the brethren, and went to Damascus, to bring them which were there bound unto Jerusalem, for to be punished.**

> **And it came to pass, that, as I made my journey, and was come nigh unto Damascus about noon, suddenly there shone from heaven a great light round about me.**

> And I fell unto the ground, and heard a voice saying unto me, Saul, Saul, why persecutest thou me? [Acts 22:5-7].

Paul is telling them his experience.

> And I answered, Who art thou, Lord? And he said unto me, I am Jesus of Nazareth, whom thou persecutest [Acts 22:8].

I think you could have heard a pin drop in that crowd now.

> And they that were with me saw indeed the light, and were afraid; but they heard not the voice of him that spake to me [Acts 22:9].

I want to stop to notice something here. If you will recall where we read about the conversion of Saul of Tarsus, it says, "And the men which journeyed with him stood speechless, hearing a voice, but seeing no man" (Acts 9:7). Here Paul says, "But they heard not the voice of him that spake to me." This looks like it might be a contradiction, and it is something which the critic likes to pounce on.

Actually, there is no contradiction at all. The men heard a voice—they heard the sound, but they did not understand what the voice said nor did they know whose voice it was. They simply heard a voice.

> And I said, what shall I do, Lord? And the Lord said unto me, Arise, and go into Damascus; and there it shall be told thee of all things which are appointed for thee to do.
>
> And when I could not see for the glory of that light, being led by the hand of them that were with me, I came into Damascus.
>
> And one Ananias, a devout man according to the law, having a good report of all the Jews which dwelt there,

> Came unto me, and stood, and said unto me, Brother Saul, receive thy sight. And the same hour I looked up upon him.
>
> And he said, The God of our fathers hath chosen thee, that thou shouldest know his will, and see that Just One, and shouldest hear the voice of his mouth.
>
> For thou shalt be his witness unto all men of what thou has seen and heard [Acts 22:10–15].

Notice that Paul had been given a private interview with the Lord Jesus. I believe that the Lord talked with him and taught him when he spent time out on that Arabian desert.

> And now why tarriest thou? arise, and be baptized, and wash away thy sins, calling on the name of the Lord.
>
> And it came to pass, that, when I was come again to Jerusalem, even while I prayed in the temple, I was in a trance;
>
> And saw him saying unto me, Make haste, and get thee quickly out of Jerusalem: for they will not receive thy testimony concerning me.
>
> And I said, Lord, they know that I imprisoned and beat in every synagogue them that believed on thee:
>
> And when the blood of thy martyr Stephen was shed, I also was standing by, and consenting unto his death, and kept the raiment of them that slew him [Acts 22:16–20].

Paul never forgot that he had been present at the stoning of Stephen and actually had had charge over it. It left an indelible impression on his mind and prepared him for his own conversion.

And he said unto me, Depart: for I will send thee far
hence unto the Gentiles.

And they gave him audience unto this word, and then
lifted up their voices, and said, Away with such a fellow
from the earth: for it is not fit that he should live [Acts
22:21-22].

Paul mentions the Gentiles because he has been out in the gentile
world speaking to them about Jesus Christ. The Jews know that. The
minute he mentions the Gentiles, it is just like lighting a fuse. They
will hear him no longer.

And as they cried out, and cast off their clothes, and
threw dust into the air,

The chief captain commanded him to be brought into
the castle, and bade that he should be examined by
scourging; that he might know wherefore they cried so
against him [Acts 22:23-24].

You see, when Paul lapsed over into the Hebrew tongue and spoke to
the mob in Hebrew, the captain stood there not able to comprehend
what he was saying. The captain simply could not grasp what was
happening nor could he understand the problem. All he could do
when the mob broke into this rage was to take Paul inside the castle. He
thought that since Paul was a prisoner, he would find out the truth
about the whole matter by whipping him.

PAUL APPEALS TO HIS ROMAN CITIZENSHIP

And as they bound him with thongs, Paul said unto the
centurion that stood by, Is it lawful for you to scourge a
man that is a Roman, and uncondemned? [Acts 22:25]

Paul is being misunderstood all the way around. The Jews thought he
had brought Trophimus into the temple, and he hadn't done that. The

captain thought he was an Egyptian who was a riot leader, and he wasn't that man. Notice who he is. He is a Hebrew who can speak fluent Greek. Also, he is a Roman citizen. He now appeals to that citizenship to escape the scourging of a prisoner.

> **When the centurion heard that, he went and told the chief captain, saying, Take heed what thou doest: for this man is a Roman.**
>
> **Then the chief captain came, and said unto him, Tell me, art thou a Roman? He said, Yea.**
>
> **And the chief captain answered, With a great sum obtained I this freedom. And Paul said, But I was free born [Acts 22:26–28].**

This captain, you see, was an ex-slave. He had saved his money or somehow he got the money to buy his freedom. He has advanced in the Roman army so that now he is a captain. He is amazed that he has a prisoner who is a Roman citizen who was born free.

> **Then straightway they departed from him which should have examined him: and the chief captain also was afraid, after he knew that he was a Roman, and because he had bound him.**
>
> **On the morrow, because he would have known the certainty wherefore he was accused of the Jews, he loosed him from his bands, and commanded the chief priests and all their council to appear, and brought Paul down, and set him before them [Acts 22:29–30].**

The captain finds that he has a remarkable man on his hands. He is a learned man who speaks Greek. He is not a common crook by any means. He is a Jew, but he is also a Roman citizen. The captain says, "I am not going to treat Paul like a common criminal. We will have a hearing to find out what the charges are against him." So the captain arranged a hearing before the chief priests and all their council.

Notice that Paul had many assets which made him suitable to be the missionary to the Roman Empire. He had a world view. Greek training had prepared him as the cosmic Christian. He was trained in the Mosaic system, which prepared him to interpret it in the light of the coming of Christ and His redemptive death and resurrection. Not the least of his assets was his Roman citizenship, which finally opened the door for him to visit Rome.

CHAPTER 23

THEME: Paul's defense before the Sanhedrin

Paul is now a prisoner, and we will follow his life as a prisoner. From this point on we find Paul giving a defense of himself and his ministry. He will appear before several rulers. Because the Jews are plotting his death, he will be taken down to Caesarea. He will spend about two years there in prison before he finally appeals and is sent to Rome.

You recall we have mentioned that there has always been some controversy, some difference of opinion, as to whether or not Paul should have gone to Jerusalem. Was he in the will of God when he did this? I contend that he was entirely in the will of God. I think that as we move on we will find again and again that Paul is in the will of God. It is true that he has been arrested, and it is true that he is having a rough time, but that does not mean that he is not in God's will.

As we go along we can see the hand of God in the life of this man. The same One who moved in the life of Paul wants to move in your life and in my life today. That is the glory and wonder of it all, friend. Right down here where you and I walk in a commonplace way, God is moving in our lives. In one way we are living a very humble existence and many of us today have a very simple, routine life. Yet God is concerned and interested in us. God wants to give us that leading and guiding that you and I need for today in the complexity that faces us in our contemporary culture. Believe me, we need that help today. There is no question that we need God on the scene.

A great many people go to the extremes today. They are trying to have some great emotional or revolutionary experience such as Paul had. I don't think that we need to do that. As a matter of fact, I doubt that you or I will have some great experience. It is by simple faith that one comes to Christ. We are to trust Him and to walk with Him. He will give the leading, the guidance, and direction in our everyday lives.

We have seen how the Roman captain arrested Paul and put him in prison and was going to beat him. He refrained from doing that when he learned that Paul was a Roman citizen. He was amazed to find that Paul was a Jew who could speak Greek and was a Roman citizen. Paul was a highly educated, cosmopolitan gentleman.

Now the Sanhedrin, composed of the religious rulers, wants to try him. Paul makes a futile attempt here to explain his position and his conduct to the Sanhedrin. The Lord encourages Paul. Then we see that the plot to murder Paul leads to his transfer to Caesarea for trial before Felix. This is a remarkable section and a very thrilling account of the experiences of Paul as a prisoner for Jesus Christ.

PAUL'S DEFENSE BEFORE THE SANHEDRIN

And Paul, earnestly beholding the council, said, Men and brethren, I have lived in all good conscience before God until this day.

And the high priest Ananias commanded them that stood by him to smite him on the mouth [Acts 23:1–2].

Paul is before the Sanhedrin. The chief priest and the council are there. The rudeness of the high priest is appalling. He was not about to let Paul speak until he was ready to hear him.

Then said Paul unto him, God shall smite thee, thou whited wall: for sittest thou to judge me after the law, and commandest me to be smitten contrary to the law? [Acts 23:3].

Under Roman law no man was to be punished until judgment had been handed in. Just because a man is arrested and accused of a certain crime does not grant liberty to those who had arrested him to abuse him. In that day the Roman law actually granted a great deal of justice. However, this incident and the trial of Jesus make us recognize that even the Roman law could be twisted and turned. Justice is dependent upon the one who is executing the law.

In our day there are a great many people who feel that if we change our form of government, or at least if we change our party from the one that is in power—whichever it may be—this will give us a solution to all our problems. It has never solved our problems in the past. The men who began our system of government had a great consciousness of God. Although a man like Thomas Jefferson was a deist and could not be called a born-again believer, he had a conviction that the Bible was the Word of God and he respected it. We don't find that in our leadership today, and yet we wonder why the system won't work. We think we need to change the system. Do you know what we need? We need to change men's hearts. It is man that needs changing, not the system.

The high priest orders Paul smitten on the mouth, and Paul speaks out against him very strongly. This should dispel the idea that Paul was some sort of pantywaist. The concept that humility makes a person a sort of Mr. Milquetoast is all wrong. Actually, humility and meekness mean that you submit yourself to the will of God, regardless of the cost. Paul is a meek man and a humble man, but he is not about to take injustice lying down. He calls this man a whited wall. "While you are judging me according to the Mosaic Law, you are breaking the Law yourself." That reveals that Paul also knew the Law. A man cannot be condemned or punished before judgment has been handed down.

And they that stood by said, Revilest thou God's high priest [Acts 23:4].

Paul didn't know this man was the high priest. Certainly he would recognize the high priest on sight. Before his conversion he had been a Pharisee in judgment. I think this is another evidence that Paul had an eye disease and didn't see too well. As we go into the Epistles, we will find other statements which indicate that Paul had trouble with his vision.

Then said Paul, I wist not, brethren, that he was the high priest: for it is written, Thou shalt not speak evil of the ruler of thy people [Acts 23:5].

Paul knew the Law. He knew every detail of it. He knew that the Law said that rulers were to be respected.

This is something else that we have forgotten today. I personally believe that the president of the United States, regardless of who he is or how bad he is, ought never to be made a subject of a cartoon. He should not be ridiculed because of the position he holds. We should respect the office. We as human beings need to respect authority. Paul wrote: "Render therefore to all their dues: tribute to whom tribute is due; custom to whom custom; fear to whom fear; honour to whom honour" (Rom. 13:7). It is interesting that he wrote this at a time when Nero was on the throne in Rome, and Nero was a madman.

> But when Paul perceived that the one part were Saddu-
> cees, and the other Pharisees, he cried out in the coun-
> cil, Men and brethren, I am a Pharisee, the son of a
> Pharisee: of the hope and resurrection of the dead I am
> called in question [Acts 23:6].

We are getting more of Paul's background. His father had also been a Pharisee, probably a wealthy and influential man.

Paul uses the discord between two parties to further his own defense. The issue here is not the resurrection of Jesus Christ. It is simply that the Pharisees believed in the resurrection of the dead and had this hope, while the Sadducees did not. So Paul turns the trial into a theological argument between the "fundamentalists" and the "liberals." That is easy to do. There never has been a time when you couldn't get these two groups at each other's throats! That is what Paul is doing here.

> And when he had so said, there arose a dissension be-
> tween the Pharisees and the Sadducees: and the multi-
> tude was divided.

> For the Sadducees say that there is no resurrection, nei-
> ther angel, nor spirit: but the Pharisees confess both.

And there arose a great cry: and the scribes that were of the Pharisees' part arose, and strove, saying, We find no evil in this man: but if a spirit or an angel hath spoken of him, let us not fight against God [Acts 23:7–9].

The Pharisees now come to Paul's defense. When they find out he is a Pharisee, they rally around him to defend him.

And when there arose a great dissension, the chief captain, fearing lest Paul should have been pulled in pieces of them, commanded the soldiers to go down, and to take him by force from among them, and to bring him into the castle [Acts 23:10].

This is the first time that Dr. Luke says there was "a great dissension." Knowing how he uses understatement, I am of the opinion that this is the worst dissension recorded in the Book of Acts concerning any group. Paul's life is so in danger again that the Roman captain reaches in and saves him from the angry Sanhedrin. While I have defended Gallio's concept of the separation of church and state, the state is protecting the apostle Paul at this point, which is quite proper. So the chief captain rescues Paul again without learning the real nature of the hatred against Paul.

THE LORD APPEARS TO PAUL

And the night following the Lord stood by him, and said, Be of good cheer, Paul: for as thou hast testified of me in Jerusalem, so must thou bear witness also at Rome [Acts 23:11].

This again shows that Paul was not out of the will of God in going to Jerusalem. The Spirit of God had warned Paul that he could expect bonds and difficulties if he went to Jerusalem. In spite of this, Paul had gone to Jerusalem and had witnessed for the Lord Jesus in that city.

Now God tells him that just as he has testified in Jerusalem so he will also bear witness in Rome. This is God's method. Paul had never had such an opportunity to witness in Jerusalem before. Now God is going to give him the opportunity to witness in Rome. It is God's will that he should go to Rome also.

It is important to note that there is no rebuke to Paul from the Lord. He doesn't say, "Look, Paul, I told you not to go to Jerusalem because you would get in trouble there." Rather, the Lord encourages him. He is using this means to get Paul over to Rome.

THE PLOT AGAINST PAUL

And when it was day, certain of the Jews banded together, and bound themselves under a curse, saying that they would neither eat nor drink till they had killed Paul [Acts 23:12].

I imagine they got pretty hungry and thirsty before this was over!

And they were more than forty which had made this conspiracy.

And they came to the chief priests and elders, and said, We have bound ourselves under a great curse, that we will eat nothing until we have slain Paul.

Now therefore ye with the council signify to the chief captain that he bring him down unto you tomorrow, as though ye would inquire something more perfectly concerning him: and we, or ever he come near, are ready to kill him [Acts 23:13–15].

This is the plot to put Paul to death. It's well that the Lord Himself has made it very clear to Paul that He has a different plan for him; he is going to Rome.

And when Paul's sister's son heard of their lying in wait, he went and entered into the castle, and told Paul.

> Then Paul called one of the centurions unto him, and said, Bring this young man unto the chief captain: for he hath a certain thing to tell him.
>
> So he took him, and brought him to the chief captain, and said, Paul the prisoner called me unto him, and prayed me to bring this young man unto thee, who hath something to say unto thee [Acts 23:16–18].

Paul is exerting his right as a Roman citizen, which he has a perfect right to do. Also, we learn more about Paul's family. We see that he has a sister who lives with her family in Jerusalem.

> Then the chief captain took him by the hand, and went with him aside privately, and asked him, What is that thou hast to tell me?
>
> And he said, The Jews have agreed to desire thee that thou wouldest bring down Paul tomorrow into the council, as though they would inquire somewhat of him more perfectly.
>
> But do not thou yield unto them: for there lie in wait for him of them more than forty men, which have bound themselves with an oath, that they will neither eat nor drink till they have killed him: and now are they ready, looking for a promise from thee.
>
> So the chief captain then let the young man depart, and charged him, See thou tell no man that thou hast shewed these things to me [Acts 23:19–22].

In this way the captain is alerted to the plot against Paul.

Let's stop to note something here. I find today that there is a group of super-pious folk, very sincere and very well-meaning, which tells me I should not go to a doctor concerning my cancer or other illnesses but that I should trust the Lord to heal me. Well, I certainly do trust the Lord; I have turned my case over to the Great Physician, and I believe

He provides doctors. It would have been a simple thing for Paul to have told his nephew, "Thanks for telling me the news, but I'm trusting the Lord—so you can go back home." But we find here that Paul used the privileges of his Roman citizenship which were available to him. Obviously the Lord provides these means and He expects us to use them. This in no way means that we are not trusting Him. Rather, we are trusting God to use the methods and the means to accomplish His purpose.

PAUL SENT TO CAESAREA

The chief captain goes into action. To be forewarned is to be forearmed.

And he called unto him two centurions, saying, Make ready two hundred soldiers to go to Caesaraea, and horsemen threescore and ten, and spearmen two hundred, at the third hour of the night [Acts 23:23].

A centurion, you remember, had one hundred soldiers under him.

And provide them beasts, that they may set Paul on, and bring him safe unto Felix the governor [Acts 23:24].

This is quite an army that is going to escort Paul down to Caesarea. Is this what one calls trusting the Lord? Of course it is the captain who has ordered it, but Paul has called for this type of protection from him. Certainly Paul is in the will of God in doing this. It certainly reveals the danger that Paul was in. There is no doubt that the Jews had every intention of putting him to death.

He is sending Paul to Caesarea to appear before Felix, the governor. The Roman governors had their headquarters in Caesarea and only occasionally went up to Jerusalem. Pilate had had his headquarters there. The ruins of that Roman city are still there today. It has a lovely situation on the coast.

I can understand why those Romans would rather live in Caesarea than in Jerusalem. The climate was delightful when I was there, and I got very cold in Jerusalem.

Paul is to be sent to Felix in Caesarea. This will remove Paul from the danger in Jerusalem.

> **And he wrote a letter after this manner [Acts 23:25].**

Although Dr. Luke may have had the actual letter, when he says the letter was "after this manner" it probably means that he didn't have access to the letter but is giving us the sense of it.

> **Claudius Lysias unto the most excellent governor Felix sendeth greetings [Acts 23:26].**

Notice the formal manner of address. In those days they didn't sign letters as we do today. They put their name at the beginning of the letter rather than at the end of the letter.

> **This man was taken of the Jews, and should have been killed of them: then came I with an army, and rescued him, having understood that he was a Roman [Acts 23:27].**

The captain in Jerusalem wants the governor in Caesarea to know that he is performing his duty. He is protecting Roman citizens.

> **And when I would have known the cause wherefore they accused him, I brought him forth into their council:**

> **Whom I perceived to be accused of questions of their law, but to have nothing laid to his charge worthy of death or of bonds [Acts 23:28–29].**

It is clear that Claudius Lysias never did know exactly what the charge was against Paul. He knew it pertained to their law. Under Roman law Paul was not guilty of anything worthy of death or of imprisonment.

And when it was told me how that the Jews laid wait for the man, I sent straightway to thee, and gave commandment to his accusers also to say before thee what they had against him. Farewell.

Then the soldiers, as it was commanded them, took Paul, and brought him by night to Antipatris.

On the morrow they left the horsemen to go with him, and returned to the castle:

Who, when they came to Caesarea, and delivered the epistle to the governor, presented Paul also before him.

And when the governor had read the letter, he asked of what province he was. And when he understood that he was of Cilicia;

I will hear thee, said he, when thine accusers are also come. And he commanded him to be kept in Herod's judgment hall [Acts 23:30–35].

We will find that his accusers were quick to come down to Caesarea. They didn't hesitate to follow Paul. As we move along, I think you will detect that Paul is not defending himself as much as he is witnessing for Christ. The Lord Jesus had said he would witness before governors and rulers and kings. He is being brought before them. This is God's method. Paul is in the will of God, and God is carrying out His purpose.

CHAPTER 24

THEME: Paul before Felix

This chapter opens and closes with Paul a prisoner in Caesarea. As we have seen, he was brought here secretly from Jerusalem to elude the Jews who had plotted his murder.

Candidly, Paul had failed in gaining the sympathies of his brethren for the gospel ministry in which he was engaged. I suspect that this was a time of mental depression and discouragement for him, because the Lord came to him in the night to give him encouragement (Acts 23:11). He told His faithful servant that he would witness to Him in Rome also. The Lord did not promise him that it would be easy. Many trying experiences and hardships were immediately before him. In fact, from here to his final martyrdom there was nothing but peril and danger—actually that had been the pattern since the day he was let down in a basket over the wall at Damascus.

In this chapter we will learn that the high priest Ananias and the elders come down from Jerusalem to accuse Paul before Felix. Paul is accused of sedition, rebellion, and profaning the temple.

PAUL BEFORE FELIX

And after five days Ananias the high priest descended with the elders, and with a certain orator named Tertullus, who informed the governor against Paul [Acts 24:1].

The accusers didn't waste time. They came down after five days in order to press charges against Paul. They brought with them a man named Tertullus who would act as the prosecuting attorney. He was a clever and well-prepared man. The charge he brought was very well prepared, too. It was brief and to the point. I think he did the best he could with the charges he had.

> And when he was called forth, Tertullus began to ac-
> cuse him, saying, Seeing that by thee we enjoy great
> quietness, and that very worthy deeds are done unto this
> nation by thy providence [Acts 24:2].

He starts out with flattery in his address to Felix. This had nothing in
the world to do with the charge against Paul.

> We accept it always, and in all places, most noble Felix,
> with all thankfulness [Acts 24:3].

Believe me, he is really buttering up the governor.

> Notwithstanding, that I be not further tedious unto thee,
> I pray thee that thou wouldest hear us of thy clemency a
> few words.

> For we have found this man a pestilent fellow, and a
> mover of sedition among all the Jews throughout the
> world, and a ringleader of the sect of the Nazarenes
> [Acts 24:4–5].

He calls Paul a mover of sedition. He couldn't prove that, of course.

> Who also hath gone about to profane the temple: whom
> we took, and would have judged according to our law.

> But the chief captain Lysias came upon us, and with
> great violence took him away out of our hands,

> Commanding his accusers to come unto thee: by exam-
> ining of whom thyself mayest take knowledge of all
> these things, whereof we accuse him.

> And the Jews also assented, saying that these things
> were so [Acts 24:6–9].

The "Jews" are the religious rulers who came down to press charges.
Notice he makes subtle insinuations about the way the chief cap-

tain handled the case. He cannot charge him with dereliction of duty, but there is a faint breath of criticism to the governor. He says the Jews could have handled this case adequately themselves. He has nothing but flattery for Felix, unjust charges against Paul, and subtle insinuations against Claudius Lysias.

So the charges against Paul are that he is a mover of sedition, he is a leader of a rebellious sect, and he has profaned the temple. Tertullus presents these charges for the religious rulers. Now Paul makes his defense before Felix.

Then Paul, after that the governor had beckoned unto him to speak, answered, Forasmuch as I know that thou hast been of many years a judge unto this nation, I do the more cheerfully answer for myself:

Because that thou mayest understand, that there are yet but twelve days since I went up to Jerusalem for to worship [Acts 24:10–11].

Paul is saying that he is delighted to present his case before Felix. He knows that Felix has been a judge of the people for a long time, which means that Felix understands their customs. So what Paul is going to say will not be something that will be strange or foreign to Felix.

And they neither found me in the temple disputing with any man, neither raising up the people, neither in the synagogues, nor in the city:

Neither can they prove the things whereof they now accuse me.

But this I confess unto thee, that after the way which they call heresy, so worship I the God of my fathers, believing all things which are written in the law and in the prophets [Acts 24:12–14].

Since Felix understands the customs of the Jews, Paul tells him that he went up to Jerusalem to worship according to their custom. In substance he says, "I am in agreement with my nation. Only I must confess that the way in which I worship God is to them heresy." But Paul makes it clear that the way he worships is according to the message to the fathers, that is, the Old Testament.

> **And have hope toward God, which they themselves also allow, that there shall be a resurrection of the dead, both of the just and unjust [Acts 24:15].**

Have you noticed that the Resurrection is the very center of Christianity? It has been from the very beginning, friend. "What think ye of Christ?" is always the test. Did He die for your sins? Was He raised from the dead? Paul immediately comes to the core: the Resurrection.

> **And herein do I exercise myself, to have always a conscience void of offence toward God, and toward men [Acts 24:16].**

Paul testifies that what he has done, he has done for the sake of his conscience.

> **Now after many years I came to bring alms to my nation, and offerings [Acts 24:17].**

Paul came to bring to the church in Jerusalem the gifts which he had been gathering on his third missionary journey. I have a notion it was a substantial gift which the gentile believers sent to Jerusalem, and Paul wanted to bring that gift with his own hands.

> **Whereupon certain Jews from Asia found me purified in the temple, neither with multitude, nor with tumult.**
>
> **Who ought to have been here before thee, and object, if they had aught against me [Acts 24:18–19].**

The real accusers, if there were any at all, are not even present. The charge that Tertullus makes is that Paul had been stirring up people in the temple. Why don't the people who were being stirred up testify against Paul? They aren't there, and Paul calls attention to it.

Or else let these same here say, if they have found any evil doing in me, while I stood before the council [Acts 24:20].

"Let them tell you about my appearance before the Sanhedrin. Did they find that I had done anything evil? Let them give testimony about that."

Except it be for this one voice, that I cried standing among them, Touching the resurrection of the dead I am called in question by you this day [Acts 24:21].

He tells Felix again that the real issue is the Resurrection. The Resurrection is the very heart of the gospel message. Christ died for our sins, was buried, and was raised again on the third day. In fact, I think of Christianity as an arch supported by two pillars. One pillar is the death of Christ and the other pillar is the resurrection of Christ. Without one or the other the arch would fall.

And when Felix heard these things, having more perfect knowledge of that way, he deferred them, and said, When Lysias the chief captain shall come down, I will know the uttermost of your matter [Acts 24:22].

Felix had been hearing about "that way"; he knew the death and resurrection of Christ was being preached. He realized that Paul was the expert, that Paul was the man who could tell him all about it. So he deferred the Jews because he wanted to have another hearing with Paul about this matter. He told the Jews he would wait until Lysias could come down, and then he could get the real story about what had happened to Paul. Apparently he could make no decision from the contradictory testimony that was offered here. Tertullus was making certain accusations. Paul said the real issue was the Resurrection. So he defers judgment.

> **And he commanded a centurion to keep Paul, and to let him have liberty, and that he should forbid none of his acquaintance to minister or come unto him [Acts 24:23].**

Actually, Felix should have freed Paul. However, he was a politician, an astute politician. He does give Paul a great deal of liberty while still keeping him a prisoner.

FELIX HAS PAUL IN FOR A PRIVATE AUDIENCE

> **And after certain days, when Felix came with his wife Drusilla, which was a Jewess, he sent for Paul, and heard him concerning the faith in Christ.**
>
> **And as he reasoned of righteousness, temperance, and judgment to come, Felix trembled, and answered. Go thy way for this time; when I have a convenient season, I will call for thee [Acts 24:24–25].**

A sinner will never have "a convenient season" to hear the Gospel.

This man Felix already knew something about the Gospel, or "the Way," which is synonymous with what we today call Christianity or the Christian faith. I personally would like to see the name "the Way" restored because *Christianity*, as it is used today, is a most abused word and has lost its real meaning.

I heard a man, actually a good preacher, say the other day that we live in a Christian nation. My friend, we don't live in a Christian nation! This country is not Christian by any stretch of the imagination. We have a lot of church members, but the number of real Christians composes a small minority today.

Felix called Paul in to explain to him the Gospel which had induced this entire situation. He called Paul in "and heard him concerning the faith in Christ." Some Bible teachers caption this section "Paul's Defense Before Felix." I disagree with that. Paul was not defending himself here. What he was doing in this second appearance before Felix was witnessing to him, trying to win this man for Christ.

The scriptural record does not present this man Felix in the bad light that secular history does. I would like you to know what a rascal he really was. To know the man, we must turn to the record of that day. Felix was a freed slave who through cruelty and brutality had forged to the front. He was a man given to pleasure and licentiousness. By the way, his very name means "pleasure." The Roman historian, Tacitus, says this concerning him: "Through all cruelty and licentiousness he exercised the authority of a king with the spirit of a slave." This was the man into whose hands Paul was placed. Yet the Scripture does not condemn him.

His wife Drusilla sat there alongside him. Again secular history turns the spotlight on her for us. She was a daughter of Herod Agrippa I. Her father killed the apostle James—we have already seen that in Acts 12:1–2. The great uncle of this woman had slain John the Baptist. Her great grandfather tried to kill the Lord Jesus Christ.

This couple of rascals, Felix and Drusilla, are in an exalted position. They probably would never have attended a church in which the Gospel was preached, nor would they have gone to hear Paul the apostle if he had come to town to preach. Yet here are these two who have this great opportunity given to them under the most favorable circumstances. They have a private interview with the greatest preacher of the grace of God that the world has ever known. God gives them a private sermon. Their palace becomes a church and their thrones become almost a mourner's bench. Oh, the wonder of the grace of God to give these two a chance! The hour of salvation struck for them. The door of the kingdom was opened and they had their opportunity to enter. This is in fulfillment of the verse in the second psalm: "Be wise now therefore, O ye kings: be instructed, ye judges of the earth" (Ps. 2:10). It appears that they heard Paul with a great deal of interest. I think Felix would have liked to have made a decision for Christ. But he didn't make that decision. He wanted to wait for a convenient season. My friend, the sinner will never have a convenient season to hear the Gospel. Man does not set the time; God does.

Paul reasoned with him of righteousness, temperance, and judgment to come. This makes a very good sermon, by the way. Righteousness here is, I think, the righteousness of the Law, which man cannot attain. In other words, the Law reveals that man is a sinner, and he cannot even present a legal righteousness that would be acceptable to God. A sinner must have a standing of legal righteousness before God, and he cannot provide it for himself. So God provides it for him in Christ Jesus. That is the "robe" of righteousness which comes down like a garment over those who put their trust in Christ. That is the righteousness "Even the righteousness of God which is by faith of Jesus Christ unto all and upon all them that believe: for there is no difference" (Rom. 3:22). Paul reasoned with this man about the righteousness of the Law which he could not meet and the righteousness which Christ provides the sinner who puts his trust in Him. Then Paul talked of temperance, which is self-control. Felix was a man mastered by passion and cruelty. These two, Felix and Drusilla, great sinners, living in sin, did not know what real freedom was. Then Paul spoke about the judgment to come, which is the final judgment at the Great White Throne of Revelation 20:11–15.

Friend, today your sins are either on you or they are on Christ. If your sins are on Christ, if you have put your trust in Him, then He paid the penalty for your sins over nineteen hundred years ago. They do not lie ahead of you for judgment in the future. But if your sins today are still on you, then there is yet a judgment to come. People don't like to hear about judgment to come.

Felix and Drusilla did not like to hear about it either. But if your sins are not on Christ, that is, if you have not trusted Him as your Savior, then you are going to come up for judgment. You can close this book right now, but that doesn't alter a thing. You cannot escape the fact that you are coming up for judgment.

Very few preachers touch on this subject. Those who still teach the Bible are the only ones who mention it at all, and most preachers soft-pedal it. I received a letter form a college professor in Virginia who wrote, "I listened to you and I was about ready to tune you out when I found out you were a hell-fire and damnation preacher. But I noticed that you didn't handle it in a crude way, and then I noticed that you did offer salvation; so I continued to listen to you." Hell-fire and damnation is a pretty good subject if it is used to lead one to Christ, friend. But it should never be used alone without the message of salvation which we have in Christ Jesus.

It is interesting to observe Felix here. When Paul had to appear before Felix, Ananias the high priest, the elders, and the great orator Tertullus came to bring their charges against him. Felix could immediately see that they had no real charge. He should have let Paul go free. But Felix was most of all a politician and did not want to antagonize the Jews. He did not do what was right but did what was politically expedient. Then Felix had this private interview with Paul, and Paul apparently really touched him. Yet he delayed his decision and postponed the day.

It has been proven out in the history of the human family for nineteen hundred years that folk can keep postponing making a decision for Christ until they come to the place where they cannot make a decision for Him at all. That is the reason that most decisions for Christ are made by young people—we ought to try to reach young people for Christ. Also this is the reason a person need not think that because he is getting older he is becoming smarter. Older people just become more hardened to the Gospel. Years ago I heard the late Dr. George Truitt, a great prince of the pulpit in Dallas, Texas, tell an incident that illustrates this fact. It was at the celebration of his fiftieth anniversary that a lawyer friend, who was not a Christian, came to him. He said, "George, you and I came here to Dallas at the same time. You were a young preacher and I was a young lawyer. I must confess that when I first heard you, I was moved a great deal by your sermons. Very frankly, there were nights when I couldn't sleep. As the years wore on, the day came when I could listen to you and *enjoy* hearing you. Your message didn't disturb me at all. And you're a much greater preacher today than you were at the beginning." The lawyer chuckled about it. He didn't realize how tragic it was. He didn't realize the place to which he had actually come. "Go thy way for this time; when I have a convenient season, I will call for thee," said Felix. That time never came for Felix. That time never came for the lawyer in Dallas. That time does not come for a great many people who postpone receiving Christ.

> He hoped also that money should have been given him of
> Paul, that he might loose him: wherefore he sent for him
> the oftener, and communed with him [Acts 24:26].

He was a clever politician and also a crook, by the way. He hoped that
he would be bribed and then he would have let Paul go free.

> But after two years Porcius Festus came into Felix'
> room: and Felix, willing to shew the Jews a pleasure,
> left Paul bound [Acts 24:27].

Felix played politics to the very end. He left Paul in prison. Again we
say that Roman justice was no better than the men who executed it.
Either Paul was guilty or he was not guilty. If guilty of treason, he
should have been put to death. If not guilty, he should have been freed.
One or the other should have been done. Under no circumstances
should he have been left in prison for two years.

CHAPTER 25

THEME: Paul before Festus

Paul had been unjustly kept in prison for two years. Festus is the new governor who followed Felix. Now Paul will appear before this new governor.

We have seen Paul before the mob on the steps of the castle in Jerusalem. We have seen him before the Sanhedrin. We have seen him before Felix and then in private interview with Felix and his wife Drusilla. Apparently there were other meetings. Now he will appear before Festus. Later he will appear before Agrippa. Paul appeared before all these rulers and it must have been a tedious time for Paul, something to try his patience. However, I'm sure that he rejoiced in the opportunity given him to testify before the high political figures of the Roman Empire. Remember that when the Lord Jesus had apprehended Paul on the Damascus road, He had said, ". . . he is a chosen vessel unto me, to bear my name before the Gentiles, and kings, and the children of Israel" (Acts 9:15). Paul is moving according to God's plan and program.

Each time Paul tells about what the Lord Jesus had done for him, and he tells it with a great deal of conviction and enthusiasm. Paul witnesses a good confession of Jesus Christ. Although Felix trembled as he listened, the rascality and cupidity and covetousness of this man triumphed. He had his chance. He sent for Paul many times, but he wanted a bribe, not salvation.

Those two years that Paul languished in prison are silent years in the life of Paul. Perhaps he chafed under it all. We don't know. We do know that the hand of God was manifested in all this, and His purposes were carried out. How comforting this can be for us when our activity seemingly comes to a standstill.

PAUL APPEARS BEFORE FESTUS

Now when Festus was come into the province, after three days he ascended from Caesarea to Jerusalem.

Then the high priest and the chief of the Jews informed him against Paul, and besought him.

And desired favour against him, that he would send for him to Jerusalem, laying wait in the way to kill him.

But Festus answered, that Paul should be kept at Caesarea, and that he himself would depart shortly thither [Acts 25:1-4].

It seems that Festus understood the situation. I'm of the opinion that Felix told him about Paul's imprisonment, and I think he explained the circumstances. I'm sure he told Festus that he had brought him to Caesarea to protect him from being put to death by the Jews. So when Festus gets word from the Jews that they want Paul in Jerusalem, he says, "Oh, I won't bring him down here. I'm going back to Caesarea myself. I'm not going to stay around in Jerusalem." Here was another Roman who preferred Caesarea to Jerusalem.

The enemies of Paul certainly didn't waste any time getting to the new governor to try to get a judgment against Paul. I don't know whether Festus was actually aware of their plan to ambush the party and kill Paul. I think he was, but it doesn't really say that he knew about it. However, he refused to accede to their demands and requested instead that they come to Caesarea to bring charges.

Let them therefore, said he, which among you are able, go down with me, and accuse this man, if there be any wickedness in him.

And when he had tarried among them more than ten days, he went down unto Caesarea; and the next day sitting on the judgment seat commanded Paul to be brought.

> And when he was come, the Jews which came down
> from Jerusalem stood round about, and laid many and
> grievous complaints against Paul, which they could not
> prove [Acts 25:5-7].

Paul is again called upon to defend himself against the accusations of
the Jews. However it provides an opportunity to present the Gospel to
Festus.

> While he answered for himself, Neither against the law
> of the Jews, neither against the temple, nor yet against
> Caesar, have I offended any thing at all.

> But Festus, willing to do the Jews a pleasure, answered
> Paul, and said, Wilt thou go up to Jerusalem, and there
> be judged of these things before me? [Acts 25:8-9].

This Festus is another rascal. Paul is not only in the midst of a den of
thieves, he is in the midst of a bunch of rascals.

> Then said Paul, I stand at Caesar's judgment seat, where
> I ought to be judged: to the Jews have I done no wrong,
> as thou very well knowest [Acts 25:10].

There are some people who think that Paul made a mistake here, that
he should never have appealed to Caesar. They think he should simply
have let his case rest with Festus. Friend, don't you see that Festus was
going to use Paul for his own political ends? Festus was going to take
Paul back to Jerusalem. Perhaps Festus was receiving bribes from the
Jews who had come from Jerusalem. I am reluctant to criticize Paul. I
don't think that he made a mistake here. Paul was a Roman citizen and
he exercised his rights as a citizen, which was the normal and the right
thing for him to do. Going back to Jerusalem would have surely meant
death for him. He doesn't purposely make himself a martyr. In fact, he
did what he could to avoid martyrdom.

Friend, there are a people today who wear a hair shirt—and God didn't give it to them. In other words, they like to take the position of a martyr. I've had a number of people who have told me that I should rejoice that I have a cancer because now I can suffer for Christ and maybe die for Christ. Well, I can tell you, I don't feel that way about it. I want to get rid of the cancer. I want to live. I think a person is depressed spiritually and mentally if he wants to put on a hair shirt and lie on a cold slab. Martin Luther tried that and he found it didn't accomplish anything.

You will remember that two years before this the Lord had appeared to Paul and had promised him a trip to Rome (Acts 23:11). That's what is taking place. He went to Rome by the will of God. He was in chains—but the Lord hadn't told him *how* he would get to Rome. This was God's method for him. When Paul wrote to the Romans, he told them that he was praying to be able to come to Rome and he asked them to pray that he might be able to come (Rom. 1:9–10; 15:3–32). I believe he went to Rome by the will of God.

For if I be an offender, or have committed any thing worthy of death, I refuse not to die: but if there be none of these things whereof these accuse me, no man may deliver me unto them. I appeal unto Caesar [Acts 25:11].

I detect a note of impatience here. Rome was noted for its justice, and Paul respected authority. However, Paul is not getting justice, and so he makes a legal appeal. God intended that Paul use his rights as a Roman citizen. It is very interesting for us to observe that God leads some people in one way and leads others in another way. Some of the others could not claim the protection of Roman citizenship.

I knew a wonderful Christian man and wife whom the Lord had blessed in a material way. They had built a lovely home, a home in which it was always a delight to visit. The man told me that he felt under conviction because he had a lovely home, and he wanted to open his home and use it for Christian witnessing and testimony as much as possible. So I asked him, "Did you ever stop to think that God blessed you materially and gave you such a nice home because He knew you were the kind of a man who would use his home for Him?" Then I said to him, "You just go ahead and fall into a sweet sleep every night, knowing that you are in the will of God and thanking Him for that lovely home." Now the Lord didn't give me that kind of a home because evidently He doesn't intend for me to use my home for that type of thing.

What has the Lord done for you, friend? Whatever it is, you should use it for Him. If you are in a political position, you should use that position for Him. If the Lord has put something in your hand, use it for Him. Remember that Moses had a rod in his hand—just a rod, but he was to use it for God. That is the whole thought here. Paul had his Roman citizenship. It was a rod in his hand. He's going to use it, use it for God. I don't think that Paul made a mistake here.

> **Then Festus, when he had conferred with the council, answered, Hast thou appealed unto Caesar? unto Caesar shalt thou go [Acts 25:12].**

Festus is forced to concur with Paul at this point. He cannot prevent Paul from going to Rome to the court of Caesar.

KING AGRIPPA AND BERNICE COME TO VISIT FESTUS

> **And after certain days king Agrippa and Bernice came unto Caesarea to salute Festus [Acts 25:13].**

Festus had just come into office as the new governor; so the king comes over for a visit. I have a notion these politicians work together. They all belong to the same party.

> **And when they had been there many days, Festus declared Paul's cause unto the king, saying, There is a certain man left in bonds by Felix:**
>
> **About whom, when I was at Jerusalem, the chief priests and the elders of the Jews informed me, desiring to have judgment against him [Acts 25:14–15].**

Agrippa and Bernice stayed there quite a long time. Dr. Luke calls it
"many days." Finally they ran out of conversation. Even a king and a
governor finally run out of things to talk about. When there was a lull
in the conversation, Festus said, "Oh, by the way, I should tell you
about a prisoner that we have here. It's a rather odd, unusual case. His
name is Paul and he was arrested and brought down here by Felix.
Felix left him for me. I'd like you to hear him."

> **To whom I answered, It is not the manner of the Romans
> to deliver any man to die, before that he which is ac-
> cused have the accusers face to face, and have licence to
> answer for himself concerning the crime laid against
> him [Acts 25:16].**

I'd like to call your attention to this. We sometimes think that Roman
law was not just because we have seen how it went awry in the case of
the Lord Jesus and also in the case of the apostle Paul. However, this
was not because of the law but because of the crooked politicians. We
still operate under the principle of Roman law that no man is to be
sentenced until he he has been brought into the presence of his accusers and his crime established.

> **Therefore, when they were come hither, without any de-
> lay on the morrow I sat on the judgment seat, and com-
> manded the man to be brought forth.**

> **Against whom when the accusers stood up, they
> brought none accusation of such things as I supposed:**

> **But had certain questions against him of their own su-
> perstition, and of one Jesus, which was dead, whom
> Paul affirmed to be alive [Acts 25:17–19].**

The issue is always the same: it is the Resurrection. We see from this
that Paul had witnessed to the resurrection of Jesus Christ so that Festus knew about it.

And because I doubted of such manner of questions, I asked him whether he would go to Jerusalem, and there be judged of these matters.

But when Paul had appealed to be reserved unto the hearing of Augustus, I commanded him to be kept till I might send him to Caesar.

Then Agrippa said unto Festus, I would also hear the man myself. Tomorrow, said he, thou shalt hear him [Acts 25:20–22].

Actually, Festus was in a sort of hot seat here. The charge against Paul was sedition and for that he should die, but he had committed no crimes. Now Paul has appealed to Caesar. What are you going to do with a prisoner like that? So he asked Agrippa to help him out.

I'm of the opinion that Agrippa had previously heard about Paul and was actually anxious to hear him. He wanted to know more about the charges and he wanted to hear what Paul would have to say. So they arranged for a meeting.

It is interesting to see how this meeting was arranged by a king and a governor. Yet all the while they were actually fulfilling prophecy even though they were unaware of this. Paul is to appear before kings, as the Lord had said.

THE HEARING BEFORE FESTUS AND AGRIPPA

And on the morrow, when Agrippa was come, and Bernice, with great pomp, and was entered into the place of hearing, with the chief captains, and principal men of the city, at Festus' commandment Paul was brought forth [Acts 25:23].

What a scene this was! Wherever did a preacher have a greater audience than this man? The setting is dramatic with great pomp and ceremony. Paul appears in chains before this august company of rulers and kings. Festus is asking Agrippa to help him frame a charge against Paul to send him to Caesar.

> And Festus said, King Agrippa, and all men which are here present with us, ye see this man, about whom all the multitude of the Jews have dealt with me, both at Jerusalem, and also here, crying that he ought not to live any longer.
>
> But when I found that he had committed nothing worthy of death, and that he himself hath appealed to Augustus, I have determined to send him.
>
> Of whom I have no certain thing to write unto my lord. Wherefore I have brought him forth before you, and specially before thee, O king Agrippa, that, after examination had, I might have somewhat to write.
>
> For it seemeth to me unreasonable to send a prisoner, and not withal to signify the crimes laid against him [Acts 25:24–27].

Paul uses this opportunity to preach one of the greatest sermons ever recorded.

CHAPTER 26

THEME: Paul before Agrippa

This testimony of Paul is not a defense of himself. It is a declaration of the Gospel with the evident purpose of winning Agrippa and the others present to Christ. This is a dramatic scene, and this chapter is one of the greatest pieces of literature, either secular or inspired.

This chapter was marvelous to me even before I was saved. When I was a young man, I was connected with a little theater. You know that everybody at some time wants to be an actor, and I had the foolish notion that I could become one. The director suggested that I memorize chapter 26 of the Book of Acts. She didn't give me the Bible, but this chapter was printed in some other book and I memorized it from that. I must say that it has always had a tremendous effect upon me.

PAUL'S TESTIMONY BEFORE AGRIPPA

Then Agrippa said unto Paul, Thou art permitted to speak for thyself. Then Paul stretched forth the hand, and answered for himself [Acts 26:1].

The appearance of Paul before Agrippa is, in my judgment, the high point in the entire ministry of this apostle. It is a fulfillment of the prophecy that he should appear before kings and rulers. Undoubtedly it was God's will that he should come before King Agrippa. I have already indicated that this made a profound impression on me when I memorized it. I must confess that it had some effect upon my decision later on to study for the ministry.

There are several features about this chapter that we ought to note before we get into Paul's message before King Agrippa. First of all, I want to make it clear again that Paul is not on trial. This is not a court trial. Paul is not making a defense before Agrippa. He is preaching the Gospel. In view of the fact that this great apostle had appealed to Caesar, not even King Agrippa could condemn him, and he is certainly out of the hands of Governor Festus, as the final verse of this chapter confirms: "Then said Agrippa unto Festus, This man might have been set at liberty, if he had not appealed unto Caesar" (v. 32). They no longer had the authority to condemn him. Neither could they set him free. They are helpless. So Paul is not attempting to make a defense. Rather he is trying to win these men for Christ.

This was not a trial, but it was a public appearance of Paul before King Agrippa and the court so that they might learn firsthand from the apostle what "that way" really was. You see, everyone was talking about *The Way*. Someone would ask another, "Say, have you heard about this new thing, *The Way*?" The other would reply "Well, I have heard some things about it. It is something new going around. What's it all about?" I would imagine that even Festus and Agrippa had some sort of exchange like that. Agrippa would have said, "I've been hearing about this but I'd like to know more about it. We ought to get it from an expert." Therefore they have this public appearance to explain *The Way*. I think this was one of the most splendid opportunities that any minister ever had to preach Christ. There has never again been an opportunity quite like this.

This was an occasion filled with pagan pomp and pageantry. It was a state function filled with fanfare and the blowing of trumpets. There was the tapestry and tinsel. The function was attended by all the prominent personages of that section and the prestige of Rome. There must have been a scramble for people to be able to attend this occasion. The purple of Agrippa and the pearls of Bernice were in evidence. There were the gold braid and the brass hats of the Roman Empire. The elect and the elite, the intelligentsia and the sophisticates had all turned out in full regalia. There would be the pride and ostentation and the dignity and display which only Rome could put on parade in that day.

Notice again how Dr. Luke records it: "And on the morrow, when Agrippa was come, and Bernice, with great pomp, and was entered into the place of hearing, with the chief captains, and principal men of the city, at Festus' commandment Paul was brought forth" (Acts 25:23).

This stirs the imagination. I trust that somehow we can picture this scene before us as we listen to the message of Paul. This elaborate gathering is for just one purpose: to hear from a notable prisoner by the name of Paul. He is the one who has already been over the greater part of the Roman Empire, certainly the eastern part of it, preaching *The Way*.

When the door of that great throne room swings open, a prisoner in chains is ushered into this colorful scene. He is dressed in the garb of a prisoner, and he is chained to two guards. He is unimpressive in his personal appearance. This is the man who teaches and preaches the death, the burial, and the resurrection of Christ for men because they are sinners and need a Savior. This is the one who can speak with authority about the new *Way*. And they will listen to this man because he knows how to speak and because he is an intelligent man. The light of heaven is on his face. He is no longer Saul of Tarsus but Paul the apostle. What a contrast he is to that gay, giddy crowd of nobility gathered there!

Festus told how the Jews had tried to kill Paul. My, how they hated him, and yet they had no real charge against him. That whole crowd looked at Paul, and I rather think that he looked over the whole crowd.

Paul is not a scintillating personality. Some liberal has called him, "Pestiferous Paul." Well, you can call him that if you want to. Maybe in the Roman Empire that is what they thought of him. Remember that the Lord Jesus had said, "If the world hate you, ye know that it hated me before it hated you" (John 15:18). This man is true to the Lord Jesus, so the world will hate him.

I do not think, frankly, that Paul was physically attractive. Yet he had the dynamic kind of attraction which the grace of God gives to a man. He was energized by the Holy Spirit. Oh, that you and I might be able to say with Paul, "I am crucified with Christ: nevertheless I live; yet not I, but Christ liveth in me: and the life which I now live in the flesh I live by the faith of the Son of God, who loved me, and gave himself for me" (Gal. 2:20).

Now let's turn our eyes from the glitter and the glamour of the occasion to the two men who stand out in this assembly: Agrippa and Paul. What a contrast! One of them is in purple, the other is in prison garb. One is on a throne, the other is in shackles. One wears a crown, the other is in chains. Agrippa is a king, but in the slavery of sin. Paul is a chained prisoner, rejoicing in the freedom of sins forgiven and liberty in Christ. Agrippa is an earthly king who could not free Paul nor himself. Paul is an ambassador of the King who had freed him and who could free Agrippa from the damning effects of sin.

We need to remember that King Agrippa was a member of the family of Herod. He belonged to the rottenest family that I know anything about. It is the worst family that is mentioned in the Bible. I think old Ahab and Jezebel were like Sunday School kids compared to the Herod family. You know the old bromide about giving the Devil his due. Well, let's give the Herods their due. Agrippa was an intelligent man and a great man in many respects in spite of his background. He knew the Mosaic Law, that is, he knew the letter of it. Paul rejoiced in this because it gave him an opportunity to speak to a man who was instructed and who would understand the nature of the charges.

As I have said before, I can't help but believe that Paul was getting a little impatient during those two years of incarceration. He had appeared before the mob in Jerusalem, before the captain, then before Felix, (publicly, then privately many times), then he appeared before Festus. Now he must appear before Agrippa. None of these other men fully understood the background of the charges against Paul. Neither did they understand the Gospel. This is true even of the Roman captain in Jerusalem. It is amazing that these people could have lived in that area, have been exposed to Christians, have heard the apostle Paul, and still not really have understood. Yet that was the situation.

Paul's plea to Agrippa to turn to Christ is magnificent. It is logical and it is intelligent. Rather than being a defense, it is a declaration of the Gospel.

> **I think myself happy, king Agrippa, because I shall answer for myself this day before thee touching all the things whereof I am accused of the Jews:**
>
> **Especially because I know thee to be expert in all customs and questions which are among the Jews: wherefore I beseech thee to hear me patiently [Acts 26:2–3].**

Paul is now speaking to a man who understands what he is talking about. Agrippa is an intelligent man, he knows the Mosaic Law, and he understands the Jewish background. Paul really rejoices in this opportunity to speak to such an instructed man who will understand the true nature of the case. Paul likewise is well instructed in the Mosaic Law, but Paul has met Christ. Now the Law has a new meaning for him. The soul of Paul is flooded with a new light. Now he sees that Christ is the end of the Law for righteousness. Now he knows that God has supplied that which He had demanded. He knows that God is good and that through Christ God is gracious. Paul wants King Agrippa to know this. There is a consummate passion filling the soul of the apostle as he speaks. I think this is his masterpiece. His message on Mars' Hill is great, but it does not compare at all to this message.

Although there were probably several hundred people present to hear this message, Paul is speaking to only one man, King Agrippa. Paul is trying to win this man for Christ.

Paul starts with a very courteous introduction, telling Agrippa how he rejoices in this opportunity. Then he proceeds to give King Agrippa a brief sketch of his youth and background. Then he tells of his conversion. Finally he makes his attempt to reach the man for Christ.

Now first of all I am going to ask you to read this entire message without interruption. Actually it tells its own story. Then I shall make some comments about it.

I think myself happy, king Agrippa, because I shall answer for myself this day before thee touching all the things whereof I am accused of the Jews:

Especially because I know thee to be expert in all customs and questions which are among the Jews: wherefore I beseech thee to hear me patiently.

My manner of life from my youth, which was at the first among mine own nation at Jerusalem, know all the Jews;

Which knew me from the beginning, if they would tes-

tify, that after the most straitest sect of our religion I lived a Pharisee.

And now I stand and am judged for the hope of the promise made of God unto our fathers:

Unto which promise our twelve tribes, instantly serving God day and night, hope to come. For which hope's sake, king Agrippa, I am accused of the Jews.

Why should it be thought a thing incredible with you, that God should raise the dead?

I verily thought with myself, that I ought to do many things contrary to the name of Jesus of Nazareth.

Which thing I also did in Jerusalem: and many of the saints did I shut up in prison, having received authority from the chief priests; and when they were put to death, I gave my voice against them.

And I punished them oft in every synagogue, and compelled them to blaspheme; and being exceedingly mad against them, I persecuted them even unto strange cities.

Whereupon as I went to Damascus with authority and commission from the chief priests,

At midday, O king, I saw in the way a light from heaven, above the brightness of the sun, shining round about me and them which journeyed with me.

And when we were all fallen to the earth, I heard a voice speaking unto me, and saying in the Hebrew tongue, Saul, Saul, why persecutest thou me? it is hard for thee to kick against the pricks.

And I said, Who art thou, Lord? And he said, I am Jesus whom thou persecutest.

But rise, and stand upon thy feet: for I have appeared unto thee for this purpose, to make thee a minister and a witness both of these things which thou hast seen, and of those things in the which I will appear unto thee;

Delivering thee from the people, and from the Gentiles, unto whom now I send thee,

To open their eyes, and to turn them from darkness to light, and from the power of Satan unto God, that they may receive forgiveness of sins, and inheritance among them which are sanctified by faith that is in me.

Whereupon, O king Agrippa, I was not disobedient unto the heavenly vision:

But shewed first unto them of Damascus, and at Jerusalem, and throughout all the coasts of Judaea, and then to the Gentiles, that they should repent and turn to God, and do works meet for repentance.

For these causes the Jews caught me in the temple, and went about to kill me.

Having therefore obtained help of God, I continue unto this day, witnessing both to small and great, saying none other things than those which the prophets and Moses did say should come:

That Christ should suffer, and that he should be the first that should rise from the dead, and should shew light unto the people, and to the Gentiles [Acts 26:2-23].

After Paul gives a simple explanation of his conduct, which was the natural outcome of his background, he goes on to tell how he lived a Pharisee, and then of the experience he had on the Damascus road.

He said, "I thought I should do many things contrary to the name of Jesus of Nazareth." The Lord Jesus has never had an enemy more bitter and brutal than Saul of Tarsus. He had an inveterate hatred of Jesus

Christ and of the Gospel. He tells how he wasted the church in Jerusalem and how he shut up many of the saints in prison. This is one reason he could endure two years of prison and such abuse from the religious leaders. He had been one of them. He knew exactly how they felt.

Then in verse 13 he recounts his experience on the Damascus road, how the Lord Jesus waylaid him, how he fell to the ground and heard Jesus speak to him. Then Paul realized he was going against the will of God. Many years later, as he was writing to the Philippians about this experience he said, "But what things were gain to me, those I counted loss for Christ. Yea doubtless, and I count all things but loss for the excellency of the knowledge of Christ Jesus my Lord: for whom I have suffered the loss of all things, and do count them but dung, that I may win Christ" (Phil. 3:7-8). A revolution really took place in his life. He had trusted religion, but when he met Jesus Christ, he got rid of all his religion. What was gain he counted loss. Jesus Christ, whom he had hated above everything else, became for him the most wonderful Person in his life.

Then Paul describes for Festus and King Agrippa the reality of the vision he had. The Lord commissioned him to preach to the Gentiles and promised to deliver him from them. That was a telling blow since there he stands before these two powerful Gentiles who cannot touch him because he has appealed to Caesar—and yet he is able to preach the Gospel to them!

Beginning with verse 19, Paul tells his response to the vision that he had. "Whereupon, O king Agrippa, I was not disobedient unto the heavenly vision." The implication is, "What else could I have done? Wouldn't you have done the same thing?"

From the beginning Paul is making it clear that *The Way* is a development and fulfillment of the Old Testament. "Having therefore obtained help of God, I continue unto this day, witnessing both to small and great, saying none other things than those which the prophets and Moses did say should come" (v. 22). It is not contrary to the Old Testament.

Now Paul presents the Gospel to this man King Agrippa—and all the crowd assembled there that day heard it. "That Christ should suffer, and that he should be the first that should rise from the dead, and should shew light unto the people, and to the Gentiles" (v. 23). I think Paul emphasized that word *Gentiles* because the king was a Gentile. Notice that he has presented the Gospel: that Christ died for our sins, that He was buried, and that He rose again. Paul, as always, emphasized the Resurrection. Friend, we should never preach the death of Christ without also preaching about His resurrection. Paul confronts that august assembly with the fact that God has intruded into the history of man and that God has done something for man. God demonstrated His love—God so loved the world that He gave His Son.

Suddenly there is an interruption. Evidently Governor Festus is on a hot seat.

> **And as he thus spake for himself, Festus said with a loud voice, Paul, thou art beside thyself; much learning doth make thee mad.**

> **But he said, I am not mad, most noble Festus; but speak forth the words of truth and soberness [Acts 26:24–25].**

It seems unfortunate that Paul is interrupted at this point. But notice how courteously Paul answers him. Certainly his calm response demonstrates that he is not a madman and he is not a fanatic.

In our day, friend, there are many witnesses, especially ministers, who are so afraid that they won't appear intellectual, but will be considered fanatical, that they do not declare the great truths of the Gospel. Friend, we ought to be willing to take the place of madmen—but not act like them. We should present the Gospel soberly as Paul did.

Notice that having answered Governor Festus, Paul went right back to King Agrippa with the question.

> **For the king knoweth of these things, before whom also I speak freely: for I am persuaded that none of these things are hidden from him; for this thing was not done in a corner.**

> **King Agrippa, believest thou the prophets? I know that thou believest [Acts 26:26–27].**

It is possible to believe the facts without them being meaningful to you. You may know the facts of the Gospel—that Jesus died for your sins and rose again—but your relationship to these facts is the thing that is essential.

> **Then Agrippa said unto Paul, Almost thou persuadest me to be a Christian.**
>
> **And Paul said, I would to God, that not only thou, but also all that hear me this day, were both almost, and altogether such as I am, except these bonds [Acts 26:28–29].**

Agrippa was an intelligent man. He answered, "Almost thou persuadest me to be a Christian." Friend, do you know that you can almost be a Christian and then be lost for time and eternity? How tragic that is! "Almost" will not do. It must be all or nothing. Either you accept Christ or you don't accept Christ. No theologian can probe the depths of salvation and its meaning. Yet it is simple enough for ordinary folk like most of us to understand. Either you have Christ or you don't have Christ. Either you trust Christ or you don't trust Christ. Either He is your Savior or He is not your Savior. It is one of the two. There is no such thing as a middle ground. It cannot be *almost*. It must be all.

Paul answered, "I would to God, that not only thou, but also all that hear me this day, were both almost, and altogether such as I am, except these bonds." Paul is saying that he longs for them to have a relationship to Christ and be like he is—except for the chains. He wouldn't want chains on anyone. This is the man who had been a proud and zealous Pharisee. This is the man who a few years before bound Christians in chains and put them to death. Now his attitude is different. He wants all people to become Christians and to have a vital and personal relationship with Jesus Christ.

One cannot help but be struck by the mighty transformation that had taken place in Saul of Tarsus. What is the explanation? It is that Jesus was *alive!* He was back from the dead. This is why Paul said very early in his testimony before Agrippa, "Why should it be thought a thing incredible with you, that God should raise the dead?" There is nothing unreasonable about that. Nineteen hundred years of man's development in knowledge in many fields makes the Resurrection even more credible in our day. Actually, it should be easier for you to believe in the Resurrection than it was for folk in that day.

Since Jesus is back from the dead, there is another and coming judgment. There is another throne, and Jesus is seated upon it. And there is another prisoner—the prisoner is you or me. Either you have bowed to Him and accepted Him as your Lord and Savior, or you will be accountable to Him in that day. The Resurrection is very important to the unsaved man as well as the saved man.

And when he had thus spoken, the king rose up, and the governor, and Bernice, and they that sat with them:

And when they were gone aside, they talked between themselves, saying, This man doeth nothing worthy of death or of bonds.

Then said Agrippa unto Festus, This man might have been set at liberty, if he had not appealed unto Caesar [Acts 26:30–32].

It is obvious that Paul is going to Rome now. We have mentioned before that there are those who question whether Paul did the right thing when he appealed to Caesar. Some feel that Paul made a mistake. I don't think it was a mistake at all.

In the Epistle to the Romans Paul expressed his longing to go to Rome. "Making request, if by any means now at length I might have a prosperous journey by the will of God to come unto you. For I long to see you, that I may impart unto you some spiritual gift, to the end ye may be established" (Rom. 1:10–11).

He is going to Rome all right. You may question whether or not he had a "prosperous journey." I have a friend in the ministry who ran a series of messages for young people (which were tremendous, by the way), and the title of the series was "Paul's Prosperous Journey to Rome." It was a prosperous journey in that it was the will of God that he should go to Rome.

CHAPTER 27

THEME: Paul goes to Rome via storm and shipwreck

This sea voyage might reasonably be called Paul's fourth missionary journey. He was just as active when he went to Rome, he exercised the same latitude, he made as many contacts, and he witnessed just as faithfully as he had on his other journeys. Chains did not hinder him even though he made this entire journey in chains. He is the one who said "Wherein I suffer trouble, as an evildoer, even unto bonds; but the word of God is not bound" (2 Tim. 2:9). Also he wrote to the Philippians that the things which happened to him worked out for the furtherance of the Gospel (Phil. 1:12).

God is in all of this, friend. The trip this time will be a little different from the others. It is to be made at the expense of the Roman government because he is Rome's prisoner. This is the fulfillment of Paul's prayer that he might come to Rome.

When Paul appealed his case to Caesar, he was moved out of the jurisdiction of Festus, the governor, and King Agrippa. As King Agrippa had said after hearing his case, "This man might have been set at liberty, if he had not appealed unto Caesar" (Acts 26:32). They couldn't do anything about it now; they must send Paul to Rome.

In chapter 27 of Acts we have the record of his voyage to Rome. What we have here might be called the log of the ship. This chapter of Acts has been considered the finest description of a sea voyage in the ancient world that is on record today. Sir William Ramsay made a study of Dr. Luke's writing, and he considers this a masterpiece and the most accurate that has ever been written. So we are coming to another great chapter in the Bible, as you can see.

Those of you who have studied Caesar in Latin may recall the account of the building of a bridge. That has always been a passage that stands out in the memory of all who study Latin because there are so many new words that pertain to the building of a bridge. This chapter in the Greek corresponds to it because there are many technical terms which Dr. Luke uses to describe this voyage.

Let's take off now with the apostle Paul. We're going to take a sea voyage to Rome. This is the final and most exciting travelog in the Book of Acts.

PAUL'S PROSPEROUS JOURNEY TO ROME

And when it was determined that we should sail into Italy, they delivered Paul and certain other prisoners unto one named Julius, a centurion of Augustus' band [Acts 27:1].

This is the beginning of the voyage to Italy. Paul, along with other prisoners, is put in the charge of a centurion by the name of Julius. I would think it safe to say that Paul was the only one of the prisoners who was a Roman citizen. Probably the others were criminals who were sent to Rome for execution. Many of them would become gladiators and would be fed to the wild beasts. In that day there was a constant stream of human life from all corners of the empire that was being fed into the mall of this public vice there in the Colosseum in Rome. These prisoners would be utterly hopeless men. What an opportunity this gave Paul to bring the Gospel of hope to this class of men. You will remember that the Lord Jesus Himself said that one of the reasons He came was to set the prisoners free—free spiritually, delivered from their sins and delivered from their guilt.

This centurion, Julius, was a very courteous pagan, as we shall see.

And entering into a ship of Adramyttium, we launched, meaning to sail by the coasts of Asia; one Aristarchus, a Macedonian of Thessalonica, being with us [Acts 27:2].

Again, it will be a help if you will follow this voyage on a map. You will notice that now they are going up the coast of Israel. In other words, they don't sail directly out to sea from the point of departure and then arrive at Rome. The ship hovers close to the coastline and goes up the coast of Israel.

> **And the next day we touched at Sidon. And Julius cour-
> teously entreated Paul, and gave him liberty to go unto
> his friends to refresh himself [Acts 27:3].**

Sidon is a familiar place to us. Tyre and Sidon are up on the coast in Phoenicia in what is now the country of Lebanon.

Notice the liberty that is granted to the apostle Paul. I am of the opinion that here is a Roman official whom Paul reached with the Gospel. His treatment of Paul is gracious. Even the great apostle Paul needed the fellowship and refreshment of Christian brethren. None of us are immune to that. We need the understanding and encouragement of one another.

> **And when we had launched from thence, we sailed un-
> der Cyprus, because the winds were contrary [Acts
> 27:4].**

"Under Cyprus" actually means that they came all the way down south of Cyprus, which indicates they were encountering some north winds.

> **And when we had sailed over the sea of Cilicia and Pam-
> phylia, we came to Myra, a city of Lycia [Acts 27:5].**

We've been with Paul over this water before. They are sailing along the southern coast of Asia Minor, hovering close to the shore along there.

> **And there the centurion found a ship of Alexandria sail-
> ing into Italy; and he put us therein [Acts 27:6].**

If you check on your map, you will see that Myra is sort of a jumping-off place. This was the place at which they changed ships. The centurion found a ship of Alexandria, which means it had come up from northern Africa and was sailing to Italy.

> And when we had sailed slowly many days, and scarce
> were come over against Cnidus, the wind not suffering
> us, we sailed under Crete, over against Salmone;
>
> And, hardly passing it, came unto a place which is
> called The fair havens; nigh whereunto was the city of
> Lasea [Acts 27:7–8].

They were headed for the island of Crete. Apparently they were still having difficulty sailing. Contrary winds were the great difficulty for sailing vessels of that day. They passed on the south side of the island and came to Lasea, which is on the south shore of Crete.

> Now when much time was spent, and when sailing was
> now dangerous, because the fast was now already past,
> Paul admonished them [Acts 27:9].

This means that it was late in the season and that winter was coming on. They had been hoping to get to Rome before the stormy season. It is interesting to note that Paul takes a moral ascendancy at this point. When the sailing became dangerous, Paul admonished them.

> And said unto them, Sirs, I perceive that this voyage
> will be with hurt and much damage, not only of the lad-
> ing and ship, but also of our lives.
>
> Nevertheless the centurion believed the master and the
> owner of the ship, more than those things which were
> spoken by Paul [Acts 27:10–11].

One can certainly understand the centurion. After all, you would expect the captain of the ship to know more about sailing than Paul.

We see Paul under a real testing here. He certainly stands out. He makes a suggestion which, they will find later, should have been followed. The spiritual superiority of Paul is evident at this point. There is no confusion in the life of Paul, no uncertainty, no frustration. He is what would be called a poised personality. Paul knew the way he was going. "This one thing I do" was his declaration when he got to Rome. We can observe these qualities in his behavior throughout the voyage. Paul lived his life as a man in touch with God.

> **And because the haven was not commodious to winter in, the more part advised to depart thence also, if by any means they might attain to Phenice, and there to winter; which is an haven of Crete, and lieth toward the southwest and northwest [Acts 27:12].**

Crete is an island that lies off the coast of Asia Minor and also off the coast of Greece. It is the largest island and contains several good harbors.

Events are going to prove that Paul was right. Throughout this voyage the captain, the soldiers, and the sailors were depending on human speculation alone. Paul was looking to God.

> **And when the south wind blew softly, supposing that they had obtained their purpose, loosing thence, they sailed close by Crete [Acts 27:13].**

To them the voyage was guesswork. The south wind blew softly, so they "supposed." The captain was a man who looked to self and to the wisdom of men. Paul was looking to God. Later on Paul would tell these men, "I believe God" (v. 25). Notice he would not say that he believed in God, but "I believe God."

Life is a great sea and our lives are little boats. We can sail our boats by human supposition if we so choose. Friend, there is a storm blowing out there, a bit of a gale. The tragedy is that, amid confusion, world chaos, and darkness, most men are still guessing. There are a thousand human plans for building a better world. Yet everywhere we look we see failure. We need men who *know* God. It was Gladstone who said, "The mark of a great statesman is a man who knows the way God is going for the next fifty years." We don't seem to find many such men around today.

THE STORM

**But not long after there arose against it a tempestuous
wind, called Euroclydon [Acts 27:14].**

What is Euroclydon? Dr. Luke is using a very technical navigational
term of that day. It has to do with the north wind, and it actually came
north by east. In other words, the storm came down out of Europe.
This was wintertime and the stormy season. It was a "tempestuous
wind" and it is in this storm that Paul and all those on the ship with
him are caught.

Now I want to stop here to point out something very interesting.
You will remember that when Paul was in Ephesus, which was a time
of triumph for the Gospel, he expressed a great desire to visit Rome. It
was the great yearning of his heart. "After these things were ended,
Paul purposed in the spirit, when he had passed through Macedonia
and Achaia, to go to Jerusalem, saying, After I have been there, I must
also see Rome (Acts 19:21). The hour of darkness came for Paul in
Jerusalem. It looked as if he would never see Rome at all. In that hour of
darkness, despair, and defeat, God appeared to him to reassure him.
"And the night following the Lord stood by him, and said, Be of good
cheer, Paul: for as thou hast testified of me in Jerusalem, so must thou
bear witness also at Rome" (Acts 23:11). The Lord had assured Paul
that he would go to Rome.

> **And when the ship was caught, and could not bear up
> into the wind, we let her drive.**
>
> **And running under a certain island which is called
> Clauda, we had much work to come by the boat:**
>
> **Which when they had taken up, they used helps, un-
> dergirding the ship; and, fearing lest they should fall
> into the quicksands, strake sail, and so were driven.**
>
> **And we being exceedingly tossed with a tempest, the
> next day they lightened the ship [Acts 27:15–18].**

They were out there in the Mediterranean Sea being driven westward from the island of Crete. It looked very much as if they would be wrecked on the little island of Clauda, which, by the way, is a very small island south of Crete. They had to let the wind take the ship. They threw all the cargo overboard to lighten the ship.

And the third day we cast out with our own hands the tackling of the ship [Acts 27:19].

They completely stripped the ship of everything that had any weight.

And when neither sun nor stars in many days appeared, and no small tempest lay on us, all hope that we should be saved was then taken away [Acts 27:20].

Dr. Luke says that "no small tempest" lay on them. We have already seen how Dr. Luke likes to use the diminutive like this. He means that it was really a terrible storm. In fact, they did not think they would escape from it alive. It was in the storm that the voice of the Lord was heard through the lips of Paul.

After fourteen days of wave and wind, the folk on the ship felt that they would not come through alive. They felt like this was it. However, the Lord had appeared to Paul and assured him that he was going to see Rome. With this assurance Paul was able to stand out above the others.

But after long abstinence Paul stood forth in the midst of them, and said, Sirs, ye should have hearkened unto me, and not have loosed from Crete, and to have gained this harm and loss.

And now I exhort you to be of good cheer: for there shall be no loss of any man's life among you, but of the ship.

For there stood by me this night the angel of God, whose I am, and whom I serve,

> Saying, Fear not, Paul; thou must be brought before Cae-
> sar: and, lo, God hath given thee all them that sail with
> thee.
>
> Wherefore, sirs, be of good cheer: for I believe God, that
> it shall be even as it was told me.
>
> Howbeit we must be cast upon a certain island [Acts
> 27:21–26].

You can understand that this was a very encouraging word to all those
who were on board the ship. In fact, it was the only thing they had to
hold onto. Notice the wonderful testimony of the apostle Paul: "Whose
I am, and whom I serve." His confidence was in God: "Be of good
cheer: for I believe God, that it shall be even as it was told me."

It was revealed to Paul that they would be cast upon an island. We
will learn later that the island was Melita, which is just south of Sicily.
So they had traveled quite a distance across the Mediterranean from
the island of Crete. Melita is the island we know today as Malta

> But when the fourteenth night was come, as we were
> driven up and down in Adria, about midnight the ship-
> men deemed that they drew near to some country [Acts
> 27:27].

"Adria" is the Adriatic Sea. The Adriatic Sea lies between Italy and
Macedonia or Greece. Apparently they have been driven up and down
the Adriatic in the storm, passing between Crete and Sicily. They are
out in the deep, out in the open sea. On the fourteenth night about
midnight it becomes apparent that they are being driven near some
land.

> And sounded, and found it twenty fathoms: and when
> they had gone a little further, they sounded again, and
> found it fifteen fathoms.

Then fearing lest we should have fallen upon rocks, they cast four anchors out of the stern, and wished for the day [Acts 27:28–29].

Their sounding showed that they were moving in closer to the land. Each sounding showed that the water was becoming more shallow.

Perhaps I should mention here that I have heard sermons on "Four Anchors," and those anchors have been labeled about everything under the sun. Let us not fall into the trap of trying to spiritualize something which is very practical and very realistic. These men were in a ship and they were approaching land. Since they didn't want to be cast upon the rocks, they threw out four anchors. It required all four to hold the ship. If you started to guess how many anchors it would take to hold you or to hold me, you would be trying to spiritualize this passage. In my judgment, that is a very foolish way to handle the Word of God.

And as the shipmen were about to flee out of the ship, when they had let down the boat into the sea, under colour as though they would have cast anchors out of the foreship,

Paul said to the centurion and to the soldiers, Except these abide in the ship, ye cannot be saved [Acts 27:30–31].

The crew was trying to abandon the ship, you see. They acted as if they were dropping anchor, but actually they were going overboard. They were leaving a sinking ship as the rats leave it. They were doing something which they should never have done.

Paul tells the centurion that the only assurance of safety is for all to remain with the ship. Paul has put his trust in God. What a wonderful thing it is to trust the Word of God. The angel of God had told Paul that he and the men would be saved. But they couldn't be saved their way. They must be saved God's way. God's way was for them to stay with the ship. It was a question of believing that God would save them or not believing and taking matters into their own hands. Paul had told them that he believed God. And he tells them that if they want to be saved, all will need to stay on board the ship.

Then the soldiers cut off the ropes of the boat, and let her fall off [Acts 27:32].

Paul has given the information to the centurion. The centurion is beginning to listen to Paul now. He gives the command and the soldiers cut the ropes to the life boats. Now everyone must stay on board.

And while the day was coming on, Paul besought them all to take meat, saying, This day is the fourteenth day that ye have tarried and continued fasting, having taken nothing.

Wherefore I pray you to take some meat: for this is for your health: for there shall not an hair fall from the head of any of you [Acts 27:33–34].

You know very well, fourteen days of fasting would weaken even the hardiest men. Now Paul urges them all to eat. Apparently they had all fasted. The pagans had fasted because they were scared to death. Paul and the Christians may have fasted because they were doing it unto the Lord. Now they are near land and they all need their strength to make it to shore. So Paul uses sanctified sanity in the Lord's service. He uses good sense.

In Christian work we need just good, common, sanctified sense more than in any other area of life. How foolish people can be and at the same time excuse it by saying they are simply trusting the Lord. My friend, the Lord expects us to use some common sense.

And when he had thus spoken, he took bread, and gave thanks to God in presence of them all: and when he had broken it, he began to eat [Acts 27:35].

Paul gave thanks to God in the presence of them all. This again is a wonderful testimony. This is Paul's prosperous journey to Rome. Perhaps you are saying, "It doesn't sound very prosperous to me! It seems to me he is out of the will of God!" No, my friend, Paul is not out of the will of God.

Do you remember another instance back in the Gospels when the Lord Jesus put His own disciples into a boat one night and sent them across the Sea of Galilee? He told them to go to the other side, and on the way over a storm arose on the sea. He sent them right into a storm. Now don't say that Jesus didn't know the storm was coming. He deliberately sent them into the storm! He is God. He knew about the storm, and He knew what He was doing. I personally believe that oftentimes the Lord deliberately sends us into a storm. We need to remember that we can be in the storm and still be in the will of God. He has never said we will miss the storms of life, but He has promised us that we will make the harbor. And He will be right there with us through the storm. That is the comfort that should come to the child of God in the time of the storm.

> **Then were they all of good cheer, and they also took some meat.**
>
> **And we were in all in the ship two hundred threescore and sixteen souls [Acts 27:36–37].**

There were 276 people on board—so it was a sizable ship.

> **And when they had eaten enough, they lightened the ship, and cast out the wheat into the sea [Acts 27:38].**

They had previously thrown all the cargo overboard. Now they throw all their food overboard.

> **And when it was day, they knew not the land: but they discovered a certain creek with a shore, into the which they were minded, if it were possible, to thrust in the ship.**

And when they had taken up the anchors, they committed themselves unto the sea, and loosed the rudder bands, and hoisted up the mainsail to the wind, and made toward shore.

And falling into a place where two seas met, they ran the ship aground; and the forepart stuck fast, and remained unmoveable, but the hinder part was broken with the violence of the waves.

And the soldiers' counsel was to kill the prisoners, lest any of them should swim out, and escape.

But the centurion, willing to save Paul, kept them from their purpose; and commanded that they which could swim should cast themselves first into the sea, and get to land:

And the rest, some on boards, and some on broken pieces of the ship. And so it came to pass, that they escaped all safe to land [Acts 27:39–44].

Their landing could be considered miraculous, although I am not going to insist that it was a miracle. However, God certainly fulfilled His promise that Paul and all the 276 people on the ship would get to land safely.

CHAPTER 28

THEME: Paul arrives in Rome

This, our final study in the Book of Acts, follows Paul from Melita to Rome. When Paul arrives in Rome, he ministers first to Jews and then to Gentiles. The narrative is not concluded but breaks off with Paul preaching in Rome. The acts of the Holy Spirit have not been finished even in our day. The Book of Acts will end with the Rapture.

THE LANDING ON MELITA

And when they were escaped, then they knew that the island was called Melita [Acts 28:1].

This is the island which we know today as Malta. The bay where this took place is known today as Saint Paul's Bay. This is a very interesting place to those of us who lived during World War II when this island made the headlines at the very beginning of the conflict. It was the most bombed spot of the war because it was in a strategic position. At that time General Darby was the general and the governor of the island. He was a Christian and a worthy successor to the apostle Paul. He said that he had no notion of surrendering. I think it is interesting to be reading about Paul landing at this bay and to realize that General Darby had command on that same island.

Certainly in the incident of this shipwreck and the landing of Paul on the island of Melita we see the providence of God in the life of the apostle Paul. All of this is recorded for our learning.

And the barbarous people shewed us no little kindness: for they kindled a fire, and received us every one, because of the present rain, and because of the cold [Acts 28:2].

It may cause us to smile a little that Dr. Luke labels the natives of the island "barbarous people." The word *barbarian* was used to describe one who did not speak Greek. It does not imply savagery. Here we have another instance of the kindness and the courtesy of pagans. Remember that there are 276 people who have landed on this little island. Out of this crowd, many are criminals who are being sent to Rome for punishment. Yet we find this wonderful compassion and helpfulness on the part of people who are pagans. We find in the Book of Jonah another instance of this same thing when the pagan sailors tried to spare Jonah. They didn't want to throw him overboard even though he had told them they should do it. They tried to bring the ship to land but found out they couldn't do it. Sometimes pagan folk are more gracious than the folk who are religious.

And when Paul had gathered a bundle of sticks, and laid them on the fire, there came a viper out of the heat, and fastened on his hand [Acts 28:3].

You remember that at the end of the Gospel of Mark there is this promise: "And these signs shall follow them that believe; In my name shall they cast out devils; they shall speak with new tongues; They shall take up serpents; and if they drink any deadly thing, it shall not hurt them; they shall lay hands on the sick, and they shall recover" (Mark 16:17–18). I believe that these signs were confined to that time before the New Testament was completed when the believers needed the sign gifts to substantiate the message of the Gospel.

My advice to you today is not to deliberately pick up a rattlesnake. I lived in Tennessee for many years and I have never known an authentic case where someone picked up a rattlesnake during a meeting, was bitten, and was unaffected by the venom of the snake. Most of them die. Those who live through it almost die. The venom has a tremendous effect upon them.

May I point out something else. Paul did not deliberately pick up this viper. Paul was not tempting God. I consider this another evidence that Paul's ". . . thorn in the flesh . . ." (2 Cor. 12:7) was eye trouble. (I'll develop that when we get to the Epistle to the Galatians.) Paul couldn't see very well. When he picked up some sticks, there was a viper on the sticks and Paul just didn't see it.

There is another interesting sidelight to the apostle Paul that I want you to notice here: the great apostle Paul gathered sticks. These people on the island had been very gracious to them. They had accepted 276 strangers who landed there. It was cold and rainy, and they had started a big fire to help warm these people who had come in from the sea. When the fire began to go down, Paul went out to gather a bundle of sticks. This should dispel any notion that Paul was a lazy preacher. He himself tells us that he practiced his trade as a tentmaker so that he would not be a burden to the church. Obviously he was not afraid of work.

When Paul threw the sticks onto the fire, the viper would naturally crawl away from the fire. The viper not only bit Paul but actually fastened onto his hand.

And when the barbarians saw the venomous beast hang on his hand, they said among themselves, No doubt this man is a murderer, whom, though he hath escaped the sea, yet vengeance suffereth not to live [Acts 28:4].

The Greek word here for "vengeance" is *dike* which actually would be better translated "justice." "Yet justice suffereth not to live." In other words, they felt that Paul was guilty of a great crime, and justice was catching up with him. He had escaped from the sea but now he would surely die of the venom. Very frankly, I think they sat down to watch what would happen to him. They expected that any moment he would begin to show swelling in his hand and arm, then would fall down dead. They knew by sad experience, as that is what had happened to their own people. They expected it to happen to Paul.

Notice that these pagans did have a sense of justice. They assumed that Paul was a murderer and that he deserved punishment. In such a circumstance today, folk would be helping the criminal to get back out to sea to escape being punished. This incident shows that throughout the Roman Empire there was a sense of justice. Pagan Rome made that contribution to the world. Rome was noted for justice, not mercy. Sins were not forgiven. If you broke the law, you paid the penalty. Under the iron heel of Rome the world was crying for mercy. This was a preparation for the coming of Christ who came as the Savior from sin—that mankind might know the mercy and forgiveness of God.

> **And he shook off the beast into the fire, and felt no harm.**
>
> **Howbeit they looked when he should have swollen, or fallen down dead suddenly: but after they had looked a great while, and saw no harm come to him, they changed their minds, and said that he was a god [Acts 28:5–6].**

The promise of God in Mark 16:18 was fulfilled in Paul's experience. He suffered no ill effects from the venom. When folk today deliberatley pick up snakes and claim that promise as their protection, they are far afield from what God had in mind.

When they saw that no harm came to Paul, they decided that he certainly could not be a criminal but was instead a god. Although they were equally as wrong in this judgment, it did give Paul a very important contact on the Island of Melita here.

> **In the same quarters were possessions of the chief man of the island, whose name was Publius; who received us, and lodged us three days courteously.**
>
> **And it came to pass, that the father of Publius lay sick of a fever and of a bloody flux: to whom Paul entered in, and prayed, and laid his hands on him, and healed him [Acts 28:7–8].**

Paul was now exercising his gift as an apostle. He entered in and he prayed. Apparently he did not pray for the man; he prayed for himself. That is, he prayed to determine the will of God. Was this man to be healed through Paul? That is what he prayed to know.

So when this was done, others also, which had diseases in the island, came, and were healed:

Who also honoured us with many honours; and when we departed, they laded us with such things as were necessary [Acts 28:9-10].

The question has been raised whether or not Paul preached the Gospel in Melita. There are those who believe that this is one place where Paul did not preach. This is an instance where I think the Holy Spirit expects us to use ordinary common sense. Of course, he preached the Gospel. We are coming to the end of the book, and the incident is related in a very brief and blunt manner. By now Dr. Luke expects us to know what Paul would do. Remember that Paul is the man who wrote, "For I determined not to know any thing among you, save Jesus Christ, and him crucified" (1 Cor. 2:2). With the apostles, healing was God's witness that the Gospel they preached was from Him. It is very important for us to realize that Paul preached the Gospel and that the healing was the result of it. It was the evidence of the truth he was preaching. I think it can be only a normal inference that Paul did exactly the same here as he did everywhere he went.

THE VOYAGE CONTINUES

And after three months we departed in a ship of Alexandria, which had wintered in the isle, whose sign was Castor and Pollux [Acts 28:11].

Since Paul stayed in Melita for three months, it is evident that the few verses given to us here are not the complete story of his ministry on that island. Therefore, I think we can be sure that Paul preached the Gospel.

"Castor and Pollux," the sign of their ship, were gods of the Romans. There is still a pillar to them in the Roman Forum.

And landing at Syracuse, we tarried there three days.

> And from thence we fetched a compass, and came to
> Rhegium: and after one day the south wind blew, and we
> came the next day to Puteoli [Acts 28:12–13].

The storm is over. The Euroclydon, that tempestuous wind from the north, is passed. Now there is a south wind blowing again.

> Where we found brethren, and were desired to tarry
> with them seven days: and so we went toward Rome.
>
> And from thence, when the brethren heard of us, they
> came to meet us as far as Appii forum, and The three
> taverns: whom when Paul saw, he thanked God, and
> took courage [Acts 28:14–15].

Paul is now on the Appian Way. Again we see how important the encouragement of believers was to the apostle Paul.

PAUL IN ROME

> And when we came to Rome, the centurion delivered the
> prisoners to the captain of the guard: but Paul was suf-
> fered to dwell by himself with a soldier that kept him
> [Acts 28:16].

Paul apparently had the freedom to live in a house, but he was always guarded by a soldier. In fact, different soldiers took turns on guard duty.

> And it came to pass, that after three days Paul called the
> chief of the Jews together: and when they were come to-
> gether, he said unto them, Men and brethren, though I
> have committed nothing against the people, or customs
> of our fathers, yet was I delivered prisoner from Jerusa-
> lem into the hands of the Romans.
>
> Who, when they had examined me, would have let me
> go, because there was no cause of death in me.

> But when the Jews spake against it, I was constrained to appeal unto Caesar; not that I had aught to accuse my nation of.
>
> For this cause therefore have I called for you, to see you, and to speak with you: because that for the hope of Israel I am bound with this chain [Acts 28:17–20].

We see Paul following his usual pattern of approaching the Jews first. He explains to them why he has been brought to Rome.

> And they said unto him, We neither received letters out of Judaea concerning thee, neither any of the brethren that came shewed or spake any harm of thee.
>
> But we desire to hear of thee what thou thinkest: for as concerning this sect, we know that every where it is spoken against.
>
> And when they had appointed him a day, there came many to him into his lodging; to whom he expounded and testified the kingdom of God, persuading them concerning Jesus, both out of the law of Moses, and out of the prophets, from morning till evening.
>
> And some believed the things which were spoken, and some believed not [Acts 28:21–24].

We see here the kind of liberty that Paul had as a prisoner. Apparently he could have quite large crowds come to his home. However, there was always a soldier on guard to watch him.

Again we see that the apostle Paul used his background in the Old Testament to persuade the Jews concerning Jesus. As always, there was the double response to the message. Some believed, but others did not.

> And when they agreed not among themselves, they departed, after that Paul had spoken one word, Well spake the Holy Ghost by Esaias the prophet unto our fathers,

Saying, Go unto this people, and say, Hearing ye shall
hear, and shall not understand; and seeing ye shall see,
and not perceive:

For the heart of this people is waxed gross, and their
ears are dull of hearing, and their eyes have they closed;
lest they should see with their eyes, and hear with their
ears, and understand with their heart, and should be
converted, and I should heal them.

Be it known therefore unto you, that the salvation of God
is sent unto the Gentiles, and that they will hear it.

And when he had said these words, the Jews departed,
and had great reasoning among themselves.

And Paul dwelt two whole years in his own hired house,
and received all that came in unto him,

Preaching the kingdom of God, and teaching those
things which concern the Lord Jesus Christ, with all
confidence, no man forbidding him [Acts 28:25–31].

The Book of Acts tells of the beginning of the movement of the Gospel
to the ends of the earth. Remember that in the Garden of Eden man
doubted God and that led to disobedience. The way back to God is by
faith, ". . . for obedience to the faith . . ." as Paul says in Romans 1:5. So
we find in that day that some believed the Gospel and some did not.

The Book of Acts ends with Paul "preaching the kingdom of God,
and teaching those things which concern the Lord Jesus Christ, with
all confidence." The record is not concluded. The Holy Spirit continues to work today. The acts of the Holy Spirit have not been finished
even in our day. The Book of Acts will end with the Rapture, the coming of Christ for His own. The work of the church has not yet been
completed; it is a continuing story. What you and I have done in the
power of the Holy Spirit will be included in that record.

BIBLIOGRAPHY

(Recommended for Further Study)

Alexander, J. A. *The Acts of the Apostles*. Carlisle, Pennsylvania: The Banner of Truth Trust, 1875.

Conybeare, W. J. and Howson, J. S. *The Life and Epistles of St. Paul*. Grand Rapids, Michigan: William B. Eerdmans Pub. Co., 1855. (A classic work)

Eims, Leroy. *Disciples in Action*. Wheaton, Illinois: Victor Books, 1981.

Frank, Harry Thomas, editor. *Hammond's Atlas of the Bible Lands*. Wheaton, Illinois: Scripture Press Publications, 1977. (Inexpensive atlas with splendid maps)

Gaebelein, Arno C. *The Acts of the Apostles*. Neptune, New Jersey: Loizeaux Brothers, 1912. (A fine interpretation)

Heading, John. *Acts: A Study in New Testament Christianity*. Kansas City, Kansas: Walterick Publishers.

Hiebert, D. Edmond. *Personalities Around Paul*. Chicago, Illinois: Moody Press, 1973. (Rich studies of people in contact with the Apostle Paul)

Ironside, H. A. *Lectures on the Book of Acts*. Neptune, New Jersey: Loizeaux Brothers, 1943. (Especially good for young Christians)

Jensen, Irving L. *Acts: An Inductive Study*. Chicago, Illinois: Moody Press, 1968.

Kelly, William. *An Exposition of the Acts of the Apostles*. Addison, Illinois: Bible Truth Publishers, 1890.

Kent, Homer A., Jr. *Jerusalem to Rome: Studies in the Book of Acts*. Grand Rapids: Baker Book House, 1974. (A splendid work for individual or group study)

Morgan, G. Campbell. *The Acts of the Apostles*. Old Tappan, New Jersey: Fleming H. Revell Co., 1924.

Rackham, R. B. *The Acts of the Apostles*. Grand Rapids, Michigan: Baker Book House, 1901. (A detailed study)

Robertson, A. T. *Epochs in the Life of Paul*. Grand Rapids, Michigan: Baker Book House, 1909.

Ryrie, Charles D. *The Acts of the Apostles*. Chicago, Illinois: Moody Press, 1961. (A fine, inexpensive survey)

Scroggie, W. Graham. *The Acts of the Apostles*. Grand Rapids, Michigan: Zondervan Publishing House, n.d. (Splendid outlines)

Thomas, W. H. Griffith. *Outline Studies in the Acts of the Apostles*. Grand Rapids, Michigan: William B. Eerdmans Publishing Co., 1956.

Vaughan, Curtis. *Acts*. Grand Rapids, Michigan: Zondervan Publishing House, 1974.

Vos, Howard F. *Beginnings in Bible Archeology*. Chicago, Illinois: Moody Press, 1973.